W9-APJ-379

Janice VanCleave's
Teaching the Fun of Math

WILEY

John Wiley & Sons, Inc.

Copyright © 2005 by Janice VanCleave. All rights reserved

Illustrations © 2005 by Laurel Aiello

Published by John Wiley & Sons, Inc., Hoboken, New Jersey
Published simultaneously in Canada

Design and composition by Navta Associates, Inc.

The publisher and the author have made every reasonable effort to insure that the experiments and activities in the book are safe when conducted as instructed but assume no responsibility for any damage caused or sustained while performing the experiments or activities in this book. Parents, guardians, and/or teachers should supervise young readers who undertake the experiments and activities in this book.

For general information about our other products and services, please contact our Customer Care Department within the United States at (800) 762-2974, outside the United States at (317) 572-3993 or fax (317) 572-4002.

Wiley also publishes its books in a variety of electronic formats. Some content that appears in print may not be available in electronic books. For more information about Wiley products, visit our web site at www.wiley.com.

Library of Congress Cataloging-in-Publication Data:

VanCleave, Janice Pratt, date.
    [Teaching the fun of math]
    Janice VanCleave's teaching the fun of math / Janice VanCleave.
        p. cm.
    Includes index.
    ISBN 0-471-33104-X (pbk. : acid-free paper)
    1. Mathematics—Study and teaching (Elementary) I. Title: Teaching the fun of math. II. Title.
QA135.6.V35 2005
372.7'044—dc22
                                                                    2004014944

Printed in the United States of America

10 9 8 7 6 5 4 3 2 1

Dedication

It is my pleasure to dedicate this book to a group
of future math wizards, my great-grandchildren:

Tyler and Krista Bolden
and
Christopher and Makenzie Durbin.

Acknowledgments

A special note of gratitude to these educators who assisted by pretesting the activities and/or by providing scientific information—the elementary education students of Dr. Nancy Cherry, Instructor, Lamburth University, Jackson, Tennessee: Brandy Clement, Susan Crownover, Kendra Edwards, Amity Freytag, Holli Helms, Laticia Hicks, Nikki Keener, Jodie Leach, Kristen Malone, Karrinn Penrod, Brandi Phillips, Glenda Raven, Bridget Smith, Krista Vaughn.

I would like to extend a special thanks to Carol G. Cathey, a microbiologist, toxicologist, biology instructor, and an educator of three very gifted triplets: Sara, Rachel, and Jared.

Contents

From the Author

Kids love math. They are excited about finding patterns in the stars, spinning the winning number at the fair, getting the largest piece of pie, and discovering that their math average is high. In other words, they enjoy investigating topics dealing with geometry, ratio, percent and probability, area and volume, statistics, and other math topics. With your guidance, this natural curiosity can be encouraged and result in a deeper understanding of these disciplines. The investigations in this book will help you to direct your students toward developing a basic knowledge of these math concepts. In turn, this knowledge will provide a foundation on which to build more math knowledge and a love of mathematical exploration.

The prime goal of this book is to present opportunities in which to engage students in investigations. This hands-on approach encourages students to understand math concepts, gives them ways to apply the concepts, and introduces and reinforces the skills they need to become independent investigators. Although a list of new math terms is part of each chapter, learning definitions is not the focus of the book. Rather, an understanding of the terms should grow naturally from exploration and experience. Explorations in this book range from basic problem-solving and simple step-by-step math activities to challenging extensions that develop useful mathematical thinking skills.

The basic outline and objectives of each section of the book follow the standards of the National Council of Teachers of Mathematics for grades 3 to 8. Although not all the standards are addressed, the activities cover many of the basic benchmarks for this age group.

The activities and investigations in this book can be adapted for students of different grade levels by increasing or decreasing the amount of information provided. For example, chapter 3, "Division," introduces the basics of division, and for older students gives additional rules for dividing positive as well as negative numbers. Assessment of individual students is an ongoing process, but teachers need tangible materials on which to base a student's grade. For the activities in this book, I've suggested multiple methods of assessment, such as correctly answering "On Your Own" problems, as well as the traditional paper-and-pencil tests. My advice to teachers is to not let the need for evaluation of student work take the fun out of discovering math. Try to balance the free spirit of discovery with the business of recording and sharing mathematical facts.

Guidelines for Using Math Activities and Investigations Successfully in the Classroom

Review the Teaching Tips

This book is organized into five sections: Numbers and Operations; Algebra; Measurements; Geometry; and Data Analysis and Probability. Each opens with a brief description of the topic presented for the section. Together these five sections comprise a total of thirty-four chapters with more than eighty activities and investigations.

Each chapter contains two or more activities and/or investigations, and an overview giving tips for teaching them. The overview includes the math benchmark addressed by the activities, expectations of student learning, suggestions for preparing materials, and a miniglossary of new terms to which students will be introduced. The overview also includes background information and interesting facts on the terms investigated as well as one or more extensions. Answers to the On Your Own problems are at the end of the teaching tips.

Math terms used in the activities are **boldfaced** and defined in the section introductions, the activities and investigations, the teaching tips, and the glossary. Math terms in the extensions and science terms introduced in the investigations and teaching tips are in *italics*. Italic terms are not in the glossary. You may wish to enrich and expand the content of your lessons by introducing the key terms to your students.

English and metric measurements are used throughout the book. In some activities where precise measurements are not needed, English units, with approximate metric equivalents in parentheses, are listed. This allows the reader to use either the English or the metric system but is not intended to reflect precise equivalencies between the two systems.

Get to Know the Activities

Read each practice problem, then follow the steps described that explain how to solve that problem. This can give you ideas for introducing new math procedures.

All of the activities follow a general format:

Practice Problems walk the reader through problems related to the new math terms, including

- **Think!** sections, which show the step-by-step process of solving each problem.
- **Answers** to each step of the practice problem; and
- **On Your Own** problems, which can be solved by following the practice problems and answers. The answers to the On Your Own problems are at the end of the teaching tips.

Get to Know the Investigations

The investigations help reinforce the concepts explained in your lessons and in the practice problems. Read each investigation completely before starting, and practice doing the investigation prior to class time. This increases your understanding of the topic and makes you more familiar with the procedure and the materials. If you know the investigation well, it will be easier for you to give instructions, answer questions, and expound on the topic.

Investigations follow a general format:

1. **Purpose:** The goal of the investigation.
2. **Materials:** A list of necessary supplies (common household items) needed for each individual or group.

3. **Procedure:** Step-by-step instructions.

4. **Results:** For some investigations, a data table is provided for students to record their observations. In other investigations, an explanation stating exactly what is expected to happen is given. This is an immediate learning tool. If the expected results are achieved, your students have immediate positive reinforcement. If the results are not the same, encourage students to check the procedure. Be sure to tell them not to change their data. Point out that while experiments may not achieve expected results, you should always accurately record the results observed. To encourage this, you might devise a rubrics system (an evaluation that rewards students for successfully completing the investigation and not on the correctness of the results).

5. **Why?:** Some of the investigations contain this section, which explains why the results were achieved, in terms students will understand. Students are introduced to new math and/or science terms as they work their way through the investigation. The new math terms not introduced in a previous activity appear here in **boldface** and are defined in the "Why?" section of the investigation. Any new science terms appear in *italics* and are defined in the "Why?" section. All the math terms from the thirty-four chapters are included in the glossary, at the back of the book. Both the boldfaced math as well as the italicized science terms appear in the index, at the back of the book.

Collect and Organize Supplies Well Ahead of Time

You will be less frustrated and more successful if you have all the necessary materials for the investigations ready for instant use. Decide whether the students will be doing the investigation individually or in groups, and calculate from that how much of each material you will need for the class. I prefer to designate a place in the classroom where the supplies will be placed each time an activity or investigation is scheduled. I separate the materials and put each type of material in its own box or area of the table. I also provide boxes or trays for the students to use to carry the materials to their work area. You may want to have your students help gather and organize supplies.

Set Up Collaborative Teams and Assign Jobs

Most investigations can be performed individually. But forming students into teams to conduct investigations helps you manage the class and provides the best opportunity for them to learn not just the math but also how to work together. Groups of four are ideal, but smaller or larger groups also are acceptable, and in some cases may be preferable. Each group works as a team to collect and analyze data, but reports may be group or individual efforts. Not only does collaboration enhance student learning, but also working in groups reduces the number of supplies needed. Assign each group member a job or allow the group to decide who does which job. This will make group investigation time both a fun-filled adventure for the students and a time you look forward to as one of the easiest and most organized periods of the day.

Suggested Team Job Titles and Duties

DIRECTOR This team member leads the group investigation. The director is the facilitator, but each child should do part of the investigation. The director determines what part of the work each group member performs. The director also can be the one to report problems to you that the group might be having. One way of notifying you of the group's progress is to use three colored cups stacked on top of each other. The top color indicates the need of the group: red (need help immediately), yellow (we have a question when you have time), green (all is well).

SUPPLY MANAGER This team member will pick up needed supplies for the investigation from the supply table and return any unused supplies to the table at the end of the work period. Each supply manager will need a copy of the materials list for the assignment. It helps to have all the supply managers assemble in front of the supply table at the same time so you can identify the materials to them and give any special instructions for transporting and using the materials. The supply manager and the waste manager might be the only students allowed to move around the room.

RECORDER This team member records the observations made by the group. This can be in the form of drawings and/or written data. If individual record keeping is required, the recorder can collect any papers that are to be turned in by the group and hand them in.

WASTE MANAGER This team member is responsible for discarding all used materials in their proper place. The waste manager also should make sure that the work area is clean and ready for the next classroom activity. The waste manager also could be the timekeeper. It is important to complete the investigation so there is ample time for cleanup.

Supervise the Investigations

Instruct your students to read through the procedure of an investigation before beginning and to follow each step very carefully. For investigations, they need to be encouraged never to skip or add steps. Emphasize that safety is of the utmost importance and that the instructions should be followed exactly. For some investigations you may want to demonstrate all or part of the procedure before the students start on their own. You might stop short of showing the final step so the students experience seeing the results for the first time themselves.

Help Students Analyze the Results of the Investigations

As noted previously, it is best if you perform investigations yourself in advance so you know what to expect. Then if the students' results are not the same as those described in the investigation, you will be better prepared to help them figure out what might have gone wrong. First go over the procedure, step-by-step, with the individual or group to make sure that no steps were left out. If all the steps were completed, try asking the students leading questions. The students can then provide their hypotheses as to why the results were not achieved. Analyze the materials. I like to ask questions such as "Do you think exact angles make a difference?" or "Does the

weight of the paper affect the results?" While I prefer to brainstorm with students, sometimes I just have the group reread the instructions and redo the investigation. This provides the opportunity to point out to students that mathematicians check their work to confirm their results. When the results do work out, refer to the teaching tips and to the "Why?" section in the investigation to help you provide math explanations as well as any science connections.

Encourage Students to Report Investigation Results

Now's the time to point out that while learning math is a great individual accomplishment, it's also important to be able to communicate this knowledge through accurate, understandable documentation. You can assign the students individual reports or a group report to be written by the recorder, with input from the whole group. Reports for investigations can range from simple drawings representing the results of the investigation to written reports that summarize the procedure and data and give a conclusion that explains why the results were achieved. Combined class results can be written on a chalkboard and used later for class discussion, as well as to introduce data collection and organization techniques.

Make Suggestions for Further Investigations

The extension section of the teaching tips provides ideas for more advanced studies related to the investigations. Some suggestions link the investigation to other curricula, such as science and art.

Numbers and Operations

A **number** is a symbol used to represent a **quantity** (an amount). **Operations** are processes that are performed on numbers. Operations and **operational symbols** (figures representing math operations) include addition (+), subtraction (–), multiplication (×), and division (÷). An understanding of operations and the order in which they are to be performed gives kids the tools they will need later to discover the value of unknown variables in algebraic equations. Since some mathematical problems require more calculations than others, the use of a technological tool—the calculator—can speed up the process of finding the answer. The common operations of addition, subtraction, multiplication, and division are needed to solve problems containing fractions as well as to find unknown variables in algebraic equations.

Addition and Subtraction

TEACHING TIPS

Benchmarks

By the end of grade 5, students should be able to
- Demonstrate an understanding of operation patterns and properties.
- Use addition and subtraction to solve problems connected to everyday experiences.

By the end of grade 8, students should be able to
- Represent operations with models, words, and numbers.
- Compare and order integers.

In this chapter, students are expected to
- Use number lines to evaluate addition and subtraction expressions.
- Analyze word problems to choose an operation and write and evaluate an expression for the problem.

Preparing the Materials

Activity 1: Addition and Subtraction
- Make a copy of the Addition and Subtraction activity sheet for each student.

Activity 2: Problem Solving
- Make a copy of the Problem Solving activity sheet for each student.

Presenting the Math Concepts

1. Introduce the new terms:

   addends Numbers that are added together.

   addition The operation of adding together two or more numbers called addends, which are combined into a resulting number called the sum.

   analyze To separate information into individual parts, examine those parts, and organize them to solve a problem.

   commutative property for addition When numbers are added, the order of the addends may be changed without changing the sum.

   equal (=) Symbol used to compare equal numbers or expressions.

   equation A mathematical sentence that uses an equal symbol to show that two expressions are equal.

   expression Numbers or letters or numbers and letters combined with one or more operational symbols.

   inverse operations Operations that undo each other. Addition and subtraction are inverse operations.

   number line A line divided into equal parts with one point chosen as the 0 point, or origin.

   numerical expression Numbers combined with one or more operational symbols.

   operations Processes such as addition and subtraction that are performed on numbers.

   subtraction The operation that involves finding the difference between two numbers.

   sum The number that is the result of adding two or more addends.

   whole numbers Counting numbers and 0.

   word problem A math problem using only words; a problem written in sentence form that needs to be solved using math.

2. Explore the new terms:
   - Whole numbers are counting numbers and 0, which include 0, 1, 2, 3, 4, . . .
   - Sometimes commas are used to write whole numbers with more than three digits to make the number easier to read. To place a comma in a whole number, count digits from the right-hand end and place a comma after every three digits. For example, the whole number 2307456 can be written as 2,307,456.
   - Commas are also used when words are used to name a number. Thus, the name of 2,307,456 would be two million, three hundred seven thousand, four hundred fifty-six.
   - The symbol for the operation of addition is the plus sign (+).
   - The symbol for the operation of subtraction is the minus sign (−).
   - Addition and subtraction are inverse operations, which means that if you start with any number and then add and subtract the same number to it, the result is the original number. For example, if you begin with the number 10, add 4, and then subtract 4, the result is 10. $10 + 4 − 4 = 10$.
   - The commutative property for addition for real numbers a and b would be expressed as $a + b = b + a$.

- Examples of numeral expressions are 3 + 4 and 5 + 4 − 2.
- An equation uses the symbol = to compare equal numbers or expressions. For example: 2 + 3 = 5 or 2 + 3 = 4 + 1.
- To solve a word problem, you must first analyze it to determine what you know (the facts), what you want to know, and what operations are needed. You then write an expression in sentence form to find the answer.

Number Line

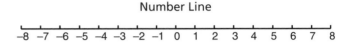

1. (−2) + (−1)   **Answer: (−3)**

2. 6 + (−4)   **Answer: (2)**

3. 7 + (−2) + (−4)   **Answer: (1)**

4. 4 + (−2) + 1 + (−5)   **Answer: (−2)**

5. (+3) + (−2) + (−6)   **Answer: (−5)**

ANSWERS

EXTENSION

1. Introduce the terms *negative numbers*, *positive numbers*, and *signed numbers*. Negative numbers are numbers with a value less than 0 and are found to the left of 0 on a horizontal number line. Positive numbers have a value geater than 0 and are found to the right of 0 on a horizontal number line. Signed numbers are numbers with a positive or negative sign. Negative numbers must have a negative sign, such as −5. But positive numbers can be written with or without a positive sign, for example, +4 or 4.

2. When using arrows to show addition of signed numbers, such as in the figure below, the length of the arrow represents the value of the number. On a horizontal number line, an arrow for a positive number points to the right and an arrow for a negative number points to the left. For example, using arrows and a number line to find the sum of 4 + (−3) would be:

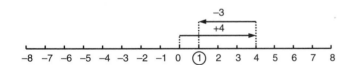

Prepare an activity sheet for the addition of signed numbers, providing a number line for each problem as shown. For each problem, students can use a pencil to draw directed arrows on a number line to find the sum of each problem. Example problems:

Activity 1: Addition and Subtraction

1.

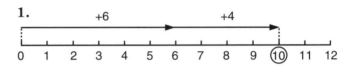

Answer: 6 + 4 = 10

2.

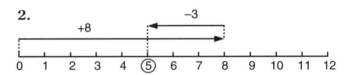

Answer: 8 − 3 = 5

3.

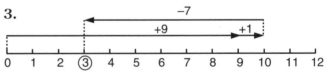

Answer: 9 + 1 − 7 = 3

4.

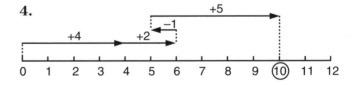

Answer: 4 + 2 − 1 + 5 = 10

5.

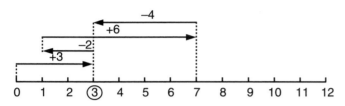

Answer: 3 − 2 + 6 − 4 = 3

Activity 2: Problem Solving

1. a. Total customers = 15

Customers given away = 7

b. How many customers did Kimberly keep?

c. Subtraction

d. 15 − 7

e. 15 − 7 = 8

2. a. Time Lacey has already spent baby-sitting = 2 hours

Time until parents return = 3 hours

b. Total time Lacey will baby-sit

c. Addition

d. 2 hours + 3 hours

e. 2 hours + 3 hours = 5 hours

3. a. Total miles to run = 4 miles

Miles left to run = 1 mile

b. How many miles has Ginger left to run?

c. Subtraction

d. 4 miles − 1 mile

e. 4 miles − 1 mile = 3 miles

4. a. Money paid to cut lawn = $15.00

Money paid to trim hedges = $10.00

Money paid to rake leaves = $5.00

b. How much did Travis earn in all?

c. Addition

d. $15.00 + $10.00 + $5.00

e. $15.00 + $10.00 + $5.00 = $30.00

Addition and Subtraction

Operations are processes that are performed on numbers, including addition and subtraction. **Addition** is the operation of adding together two or more numbers called **addends**, which are combined into a resulting number called the **sum**. You can change the order of the addends without changing the sum. This property of addition is called the **commutative property for addition**. **Subtraction** is an operation that involves finding the difference between two numbers. Since addition is an operation that adds and subtraction is an operation that takes away, they are **inverse operations**, and they undo each other. A **number line**, which is a line divided into equal parts in which all points correspond to a number, can be used to show that addition and subtraction are inverse operations. An **expression** consists of numbers or letters or numbers and letters combined with one or more operational symbols. A **numerical expression** is an expression of numbers combined with one or more symbols. The **equal (=)** symbol is used to show that numbers or expressions are equal. An **equation** is a mathematical sentence that uses an equal symbol to show that two expressions are equal. In this activity **whole numbers**, which are counting numbers and 0, will be used.

Practice Problems

1. Use a number line to find the sum of $4 + 5$.

Think!

- $4 + 5$ is an expression involving addition.
- Addition is represented on a number line by arrows that move to the right.
- Begin the first arrow at a point above the 0 on the number line. Use a pencil and ruler to draw the 4 arrow going toward the right. The length of the arrow is 4 divisions to the right on the number line, from 0 to 4. The head of the arrow is above the 4 on the number line.
- Starting at the 4 on the number line, count to the right 5 more divisions, from 4 to 9 on the number line. Use the pencil and ruler to draw the arrow from the tip of the first arrow 5 divisions to the right, so the head of the arrow is now above the 9 on the number line.

```
        +4              +5
  ┌───────────▶   ┌──────────────▶
  0  1  2  3  4  5  6  7  8  ⑨ 10 11 12
```

Answer: $4 + 5 = 9$

2. Use a number line to find the solution of $3 + 6 - 4$.

Think!

- $3 + 6 - 4$ is a number expression involving addition and subtraction.
- Begin the first arrow at a point above the 0 on the number line. Use a pencil and ruler to draw the arrow going 3 spaces to the right, so the head of the arrow is above the 3 on the number line.

© 2005 by John Wiley & Sons, Inc.

- Starting at the tip of the arrow that ends at the number 3, use the pencil and ruler to draw an arrow pointing 6 more spaces to the right. The head of the arrow is now above the 9 on the number line.
- Starting directly above the tip of the arrow that ends at the number 9, draw an arrow pointing 4 spaces to the left, from 9 to 5 on the number line.

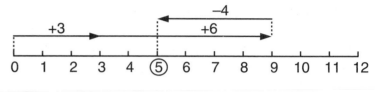

- The tip of the last arrow is above the 5 on the number line.

Answer: 3 + 6 − 4 = 5

On Your Own

Use a ruler and the number line to find the sum of each problem.

1. 6 + 4

Answer: _____

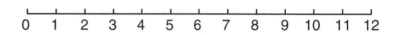

2. 8 − 3

Answer: _____

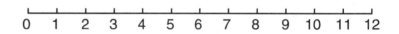

3. 9 + 1 − 7

Answer: _____

4. 4 + 2 − 1 + 5

Answer: _____

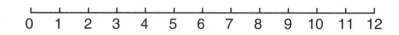

5. 3 − 2 + 6 − 4

Answer: _____

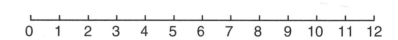

Problem Solving

To **analyze** means to separate information into its individual parts, examining those parts and organizing them to solve a problem. A **word problem** is a math problem using only words; it is a problem written in sentence form that needs to be solved using math. To solve a word problem, you analyze it to determine what you know (the facts), what you want to know, and what operations are needed. Using this information, you write an expression. You solve the word problem by evaluating (or solving) the expression.

Practice Problems

Analyze each word problem, write an expression for the problem, then evaluate the expression.

1. Jennifer had 120 stuffed animals. She had so many animals that she gave away 50. How many animals did Jennifer keep?

   Think!
   - What do you know?

     Jennifer started with 120 stuffed animals and gave away 50 of them.
   - What do you want to know?

     How many animals Jennifer kept.
   - What operation is needed?

     Since Jennifer is *giving away* stuffed animals, the operation is subtraction.
   - What expression represents the problem?

     120 animals – 50 animals
   - Evaluate the expression.

     120 animals – 50 animals = ?

   Answer: Jennifer kept 70 animals.

2. David watched television for 1 hour. His parents then left the house and said they'd be back in 2 hours. If David watches television until his parents return, how long will he have watched television?

   Think!
   - What do you know?

     David watched television for 1 hour, and will watch for another 2 hours.
   - What do you want to know?

     Total time watching television
   - What operation is needed?

     Since the question is about a *total* amount of time, the operation is addition.
   - What expression represents the problem?

     1 hour + 2 hours

- Evaluate the expression.

    1 hour + 2 hours = ?

Answer: David will have watched television for 3 hours.

On Your Own

Analyze each word problem, write an expression for the problem, then evaluate the expression.

1. Kimberly watched dogs for 15 customers. This was more dogs than she could handle, so she gave 7 customers to Lauren. How many customers did Kimberly keep?

    a. What do you know? _____

    b. What do you want to know? _____

    c. What operation is needed? _____

    d. What expression represents the problem? _____

    e. Evaluate the expression. _____

2. Lacey has been baby-sitting Jacob for 2 hours. Jacob's parents will be home in 3 hours. How long will Lacey have baby-sat Jacob by the time his parents return?

    a. What do you know? _____

    b. What do you want to know? _____

    c. What operation is needed? _____

    d. What expression represents the problem? _____

    e. Evaluate the expression. _____

3. Ginger has 1 mile left to run. If she wants to run 4 miles, how many miles has she already run?

    a. What do you know? _____

    b. What do you want to know? _____

    c. What operation is needed? _____

    d. What expression represents the problem? _____

    e. Evaluate the expression. _____

4. Travis was paid $15.00 to cut the lawn, $10.00 to trim the hedges, and $5.00 to rake leaves. How much did he earn in all?

    a. What do you know? _____

    b. What do you want to know? _____

    c. What operation is needed? _____

    d. What expression represents the problem? _____

    e. Evaluate the expression. _____

Multiplication

TEACHING TIPS

Benchmarks

By the end of grade 5, students should be able to
- Demonstrate an understanding of operation patterns and properties.
- Make generalizations from patterns and justify why an answer is reasonable.

By the end of grade 8, students should be able to
- Represent operations with models, words, and numbers.

In this chapter, students are expected to
- Use models to demonstrate multiplication as repeated addition.
- Write multiplication equations.
- Make and learn multiplication tables for numbers 1 through 10.

Preparing the Materials

Activity: Multiplication Grid
- Make a copy of the Multiplication Grid activity sheet for each student.
- Make a copy of the Multiplication Answers sheet for each student.
- Students can use crayons or colored markers to color in the squares.

Investigation: Multiplication Strips
- Make a copy of the Multiplication Strips investigation sheet for each student.
- On white card stock, make one copy of Multiplication Tables I and II for each student. Note: If card stock is not available, make copies of the pages on white copy paper and have students glue the strips to heavy paper, such as file folders.

Presenting the Math Concepts

1. Introduce the new terms:

    factors Numbers multiplied together to obtain a product.

    multiplication An operation involving repeated addition.

    product The number obtained after multiplying.

2. Explore the new terms:
    - Multiplication is used to find the total amount for a problem when a certain number of equal amounts are given.
    - Multiplication is a shortcut for the addition of equal addends. In other words, multiplication is the process by which the same number is added to itself an indicated number of times. For example, if you multiply 5 three times (5×3), one way to calculate the answer is to add five 3s ($3 + 3 + 3 + 3 + 3 = 15$).
    - Multiplication is an example of an equation, which shows that two expressions are equal. For example, $2 \times 3 = 6$.

EXTENSIONS

1. Show students how they can check the product when multiplying by 9 because the sum of the digits of each product always add up to 9. For example:

$9 \times 2 = 18$	$1 + 8 = 9$
$9 \times 3 = 27$	$2 + 7 = 9$
$9 \times 6 = 54$	$5 + 4 = 9$
$9 \times 10 = 90$	$9 + 0 = 9$

2. Define *integers*, which are positive or negative whole numbers; for example, –2, –1, 0, 1, 2. Then show students the rules for multiplying integers.
    - When two integers have like signs, the product will be positive.

        both integers are positive $2 \times 4 = 8$

        both integers are negative $-2 \times -4 = 8$
    - When two integers have unlike signs, the product will be negative.

        one integer is negative and the other is positive: $-2 \times 4 = -8$

        one integer is positive and the other is negative: $2 \times -4 = -8$

ANSWERS
Activity: Multiplication Grid

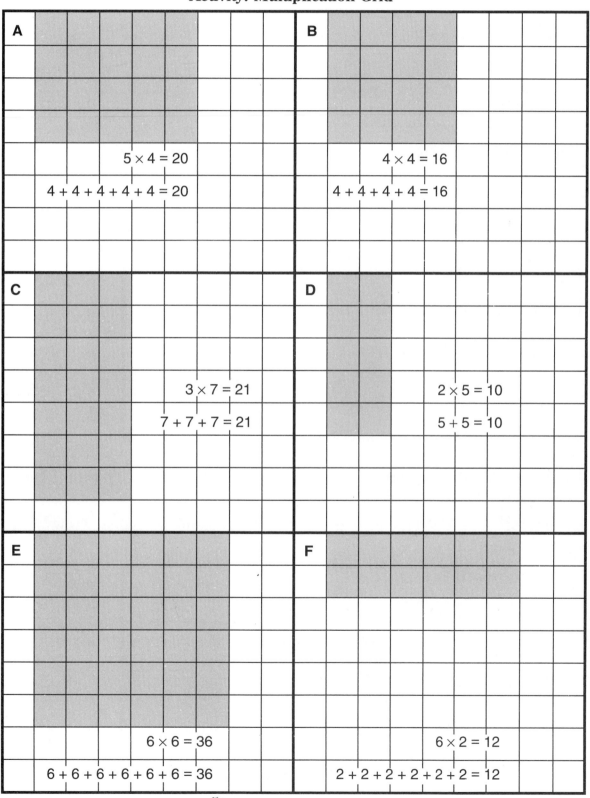

A

$5 \times 4 = 20$

$4 + 4 + 4 + 4 + 4 = 20$

B

$4 \times 4 = 16$

$4 + 4 + 4 + 4 = 16$

C

$3 \times 7 = 21$

$7 + 7 + 7 = 21$

D

$2 \times 5 = 10$

$5 + 5 = 10$

E

$6 \times 6 = 36$

$6 + 6 + 6 + 6 + 6 + 6 = 36$

F

$6 \times 2 = 12$

$2 + 2 + 2 + 2 + 2 + 2 = 12$

2 ACTIVITY

Multiplication Grid

Multiplication is an operation involving repeated addition. **Factors** are the numbers multiplied together to obtain a **product**, which is the number obtained after multiplying.

Practice Problems

Complete the following for the multiplication problem 4×2.

1. Use crayons or colored markers to color squares on the grid to represent the multiplication problem. Let the first factor equal the number of rows (horizontal grouping) and the second factor the number of squares per row.

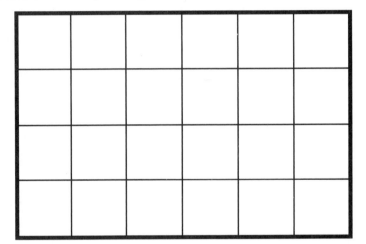

Think!

- The factors of a multiplication problem are the numbers multiplied together, in this case 4 and 2, to obtain a product.

- The first factor is 4 and the second factor is 2, so there will be 4 colored rows with 2 squares in each row.

Answer:

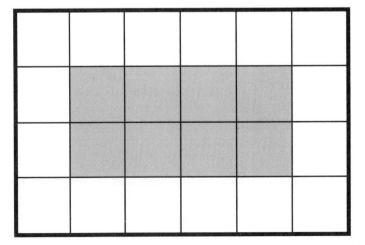

2. Write a multiplication equation for the problem.

Think!

- The product, which is 8, is the number obtained after multiplying.

- An equation shows that two expressions are equal.

Answer: $4 \times 2 = 8$

3. Write the multiplication problem as an addition problem.

Think!

- Multiplication is a shortcut for the addition of equal addends.

- The product of 4×2 is the same as the sum of four 2s.

Answer:

$2 + 2 + 2 + 2 = 8$

On Your Own

On the Multiplication Answers sheet, complete the following for these problems:
   A. 5×4
   B. 4×4
   C. 3×7
   D. 2×5
   E. 6×6
   F. 6×2

1. Color squares on a grid on the answer sheet to represent each multiplication problem. Let the first factor equal the number of rows and the second factor the number of squares per row.

2. Write a multiplication equation for the problem under the colored squares.

3. Write the multiplication problem as an addition problem under the multiplication equation.

ACTIVITY (continued)

Multiplication Answers

A								B							

C								D							

E								F							

Multiplication Strips

PURPOSE

To prepare multiplication table strips for numbers 1 through 10.

Materials

copy of Multiplication Tables I and II
ten different-color crayons
    (your choice of colors)
pen
scissors
pencil
paper hole punch
paper brad

Procedure

1. In each of the ten tables, use a different crayon to lightly color the shaded boxes, which contain numbers.

2. Fill in the blanks for each of the multiplication tables. For example, for the 2s table, multiply each number in the vertical column times 2.

3. Use the scissors to cut the tables apart by cutting along the dashed lines.

4. Use the paper hole punch to cut a hole in the bottom of each table where indicated.

5. Lay the multiplication tables one on top of the other in numerical order from 1s to 10s.

6. Insert the paper brad through all the holes and secure it.

7. Study one of the tables and try to memorize it. Then try to multiply the numbers without looking at the table. You can check yourself by looking. Repeat this until you can correctly multiply the numbers in each table without looking.

Results

You have made a set of multiplication strips for the numbers 1 through 10. Use the strips periodically to refresh your memory of the multiplication of the numbers in the tables.

2s	
	2
1	2
2	4
3	6
4	8
5	10
6	12
7	14
8	16
9	18
10	20
O —— hole	

Multiplication Tables I

1s	1											○
		1	2	3	4	5	6	7	8	9	10	

2s	2											○
		1	2	3	4	5	6	7	8	9	10	

3s	3											○
		1	2	3	4	5	6	7	8	9	10	

4s	4											○
		1	2	3	4	5	6	7	8	9	10	

5s	5											○
		1	2	3	4	5	6	7	8	9	10	

© 2005 by John Wiley & Sons, Inc.

INVESTIGATION (continued)

2

© 2005 by John Wiley & Sons, Inc.

Multiplication Tables II

10s										
10		1	2	3	4	5	6	7	8	9	10

9s										
9		1	2	3	4	5	6	7	8	9	10

8s										
8		1	2	3	4	5	6	7	8	9	10

7s										
7		1	2	3	4	5	6	7	8	9	10

6s										
6		1	2	3	4	5	6	7	8	9	10

Division

TEACHING TIPS

Benchmarks

By the end of grade 5, students should be able to
- Use inverse operations to check quotients for division problems or products for multiplication problems.
- Demonstrate an understanding of operation patterns and properties.
- Make generalizations from patterns and justify why an answer is reasonable.

By the end of grade 8, students should be able to
- Represent operations with models, words, and numbers.

In this chapter, students are expected to
- Use models to demonstrate division as sharing and repeated subtractions.
- Use multiplication to check quotients for division problems.

Preparing the Materials

Activity: Dividing Counters
- Make a copy of the Dividing Counters activity sheet for each student.
- Provide small objects such as coins, buttons, or paper clips to be used as counters.
- 3-ounce (90-mL) paper cups can be used as group holders.

Investigation: Equal Groups
- Make a copy of the Equal Groups investigation sheet for each student or group.
- Make sure each student or group has a set of crayons and a sheet of paper.

Presenting the Math Concepts

1. Introduce the new terms:

   dividend A number that is divided in a division problem.

   divisible A number that can be divided by another number without leaving a remainder.

   division An operation that tells how many groups there are or how many are in each group.

   divisor The number by which a dividend is divided.

   quotient The number other than the whole number remainder that is the result of division; the answer to a division problem.

   remainder The number less than the divisor that remains when division is finished.

2. Explore the new terms:
   - In division, a dividend is divided by a divisor, producing the quotient. In the problem $a \div b = c$, a is the dividend, b is the divisor, and c is the quotient.
   - In division, if the dividend cannot be divided into an equal number of groups, there will be a remainder. The letter R is used to identify the remainder. For example, in the following problem, 3 is the remainder: $43 \div 5 = 8$ R3.
   - Division can be thought of as:
     a. SHARING An amount is equally divided into parts. For example, 18 pieces of candy are given to 3 children, with an equal number of pieces given to each child. Each child has 6 pieces of candy, as determined by the calculation $18 \div 3 = 6$.
     b. REPEATED SUBTRACTION A specific amount is repeatedly subtracted from the whole. For example, 18 pieces of candy have 6 pieces repeatedly subtracted from it and placed in separate piles. The subtraction would be $18 - 6 = 12$; $12 - 6 = 6$; $6 - 6 = 0$. There would be 3 piles with 6 candies in each. This is determined by the calculation $18 \div 6 = 3$.
     c. OPPOSITE OF MULTIPLICATION The dividend divided by the divisor equals the quotient; thus the quotient multiplied by the divisor equals the dividend. For example, $18 \div 6 = 3$, so $3 \times 6 = 18$.
   - Multiplication and division are inverse operations, which means that if you start with a particular number and then multiply and divide by the same number, the result is the original number. For example, begin with the number 12 and multiply by 4, then divide by 4; the result is 12. $12 \times 4 \div 4 = 12$.
   - The quotient does not include the remainder if the remainder is written as a whole number. For example, $90 \div 40 = 2$ R10. To check the answer, the quotient of 2 is multiplied by the divisor: $2 \times 40 = 80$. Then the remainder is added to the product, and the sum will be equal to the dividend: $80 + 10 = 90$.

EXTENSIONS

1. Show students how to divide integers using these rules:

   a. When two integers (dividend and divisor) have like signs, the quotient will be positive.

   both integers are positive: $18 \div 6 = 3$

   both integers are negative: $-18 \div -6 = 3$

   b. When two integers (dividend and divisor) have unlike signs, the quotient will be negative.

   the dividend is positive and the divisor is negative: $18 \div -6 = -3$

   the dividend is negative and the divisor is positive: $-18 \div 6 = -3$

2. Explain to students that if the remainder is a fraction or a decimal, it is part of the quotient. For example, $9 \div 4 = 2\frac{1}{4}$ or 2.25. Remember that the quotient times the divisor equals the dividend. So $2\frac{1}{4}$ and 2.25 are correct quotients for the problem $9 \div 4$, since $2\frac{1}{4} \times 4 = 9$ and $2.25 \times 4 = 9$.

3. Explain that a *set* is a collection of numbers and that *real numbers* can be defined as the members in the set {rational numbers plus irrational numbers}. Compare rational and irrational numbers. A number that has no decimal, has a finite decimal, or has a decimal with a repeating number or block of numbers is called a *rational number*. For example, $4 \div 2 = 2$; thus the quotient 2 is a rational number. $10 \div 3 = 3.3333\ldots\ldots$ For a rational number, the dots indicate a repeat of the last number. Placing a line under or above the last number also indicates that the number is repeated; thus the quotient $3.3\underline{3}$ is a rational number.

A number with a decimal that has no repeating number or pattern is called an *irrational number*. For example, pi (π) = $^{22}/_7$ = 3.1415926535 . . . . For an irrational number, the dots indicate no repeating number or pattern. Pi has been divided by computers to 100 million decimal places, although this computation has no practical purpose.

ANSWERS

Activity: Dividing Counters

1. $14 \div 2 = 7$
   Check: $7 \times 2 = 14$

2. $18 \div 6 = 3$
   Check: $3 \times 6 = 18$

3. $10 - 3 = 7$, $7 - 3 = 4$, $4 - 3 = 1$; $10 \div 3 = 3$ R1
   Check: $3 \times 3 = 9$, $9 + 1 = 10$

4. $15 - 6 = 9$, $9 - 6 = 3$; $15 \div 6 = 2$ R3
   Check: $6 \times 2 = 12$, $12 + 3 = 15$

Investigation: Equal Groups

10 shapes
2 remaining boxes

8 shapes
0 remaining boxes

3 ACTIVITY

Dividing Counters

Division is an operation that tells how many groups there are or how many are in each group. In division, a **dividend** is divided by a **divisor**, producing the **quotient** (the answer). A number is **divisible** if it can be divided by another number an even number of times. If a number is not divisible, there is a **remainder**, which is the number less than the divisor that remains when division is finished.

Practice Problems

1. Use counters to think about solving the division problem 12 ÷ 3 as sharing. For example, if 12 coins are shared with 3 people, how many coins will each receive?

Think!

- In the problem 12 ÷ 3 = ?, 12 is the dividend, 3 is the divisor, and ? represents the quotient.
- The divisor number tells how many groups the dividend is divided into.
- In sharing, an amount is equally divided into parts. Imagine that 12 coins are divided into 3 groups, with an equal number of coins in each group. Place 3 coins on a table in 3 separate places. Continue to place 1 coin in each group until all the coins are placed. How many coins are in each group?   4.

Answer: 12 ÷ 3 = 4

2. Use counters to think about solving the division problem 12 ÷ 3 as repeated subtraction. For example, if 12 coins are divided so that each person receives 3 coins, how many people receive coins?

Think!

- In repeated subtraction, a group of objects is repeatedly subtracted from the whole. Imagine taking away 3 coins from the 12 coins until you have 0 left. Place each group of 3 coins removed in a separate pile on the table. The subtraction would be 12 − 3 = 9; 9 − 3 = 6; 6 − 3 = 3; 3 − 3 = 0.

- The number of piles of coins (4) equals the number of times each group of 3 coins is removed.

  Answer: $12 \div 3 = 4$

3. Use multiplication to check the answer for the above problem, $12 \div 3$.

Think!

- The quotient of a division problem multiplied by the divisor equals the dividend.
- In the problem $12 \div 3 = 4$, the quotient is 4, the divisor is 3, and the dividend is 12.

  Answer: $4 \times 3 = 12$

4. Use counters to show repeated subtractions for the problem $7 \div 2$.

Think!

- Take away 2 coins from the 7 coins until there is 0 or less than 2 coins left. Place each group of 2 coins removed in a separate pile on the table. The subtraction would be $7 - 2 = 5; 5 - 2 = 3; 3 - 2 = 1$.
- The number of piles of coins (3) equals the number of times each group of 2 coins is removed; the number of coins less than 2 that remain is called the remainder.
- R1 indicates a remainder of 1.

  Answer: $7 \div 2 = 3 \text{ R1}$

5. Use multiplication to check the answer for the problem $7 \div 2$.

Think!

- In the problem $7 \div 2 = 3 \text{ R1}$, the quotient is 3 and the remainder is 1.
- The quotient multiplied by the divisor plus the remainder equal the dividend.

  Answer: $2 \times 3 = 6, 6 + 1 = 7$

On Your Own

Use counters to solve the following division problems by sharing. Use multiplication to check the answer for each.

1. $14 \div 2$ _____

2. $18 \div 6$ _____

Use counters to solve the following division problems by repeated subtraction. Use multiplication to check the answer for each.

3. $10 \div 3$ _____

4. $15 \div 6$ _____

Equal Groups

PURPOSE

To show how something can be divided into equal groups.

Materials

sheet of copy paper
crayons

Procedure

1. Fold the paper in half five times. First, fold the paper three times from top to bottom. Then fold it two times from side to side.

2. Unfold the paper. The fold lines divide the sheet into 32 boxes.

3. Look at the shape drawn to the right, made up of 3 boxes in an L shape.

4. Determine how many Ls the 32 boxes can be divided into with the least number of boxes remaining that do not form an L shape. Do this by coloring each shape a different color on the paper. Follow this example:

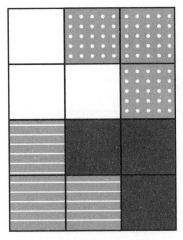

4 shapes
0 remaining boxes

5. Look at the bigger L shape, using 4 boxes, below.

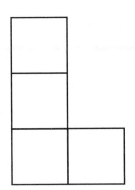

6. Turn the paper over and determine how many of the larger shape the paper can be divided into with the least number of boxes remaining that do not form an L shape made of 4 boxes. A clue is to turn the paper with one of the longer sides at the top.

Results

The paper can be divided into 10 smaller L shapes, with 2 remaining boxes. The paper can be divided into 8 large L shapes (4 boxes), with no remaining boxes.

Why?

The five folds divide the paper into 32 boxes. Dividing the paper into L shapes of 3 boxes is the same as the division problem $32 \div 3 = 10$ R2. Dividing the paper into L shapes of 4 boxes is the same as the division problem $32 \div 4 = 8$.

Decimals

TEACHING TIPS

Benchmarks

By the end of grade 5, students are expected to
- Read, write, compare, and order decimal numbers through the thousandths place.

By the end of grade 8, students are expected to
- Compare and order decimal numbers.
- Communicate mathematical ideas using models.

In this chapter, students are expected to
- Compare equivalent decimals.
- Compare and order decimals.
- Write the decimal value of money.

Preparing the Materials

Activity 1: Decimals
- Make a copy of the Decimals activity sheet for each student.

Activity 2: Comparing Decimals
- Make a copy of the Comparing Decimals activity sheet for each student.

Presenting the Math Concepts

1. Introduce the new terms:

   decimal A number that uses a decimal point to show tenths, hundredths, thousandths, and so on.

   decimal point A dot placed between the ones place and the tenths place in decimals.

   equivalent decimals Decimals that name the same amount.

   greater than (>) Symbol meaning "is greater than."

   hundredth One out of 100 equal parts of a whole; the second place after a decimal point.

   less than (<) Symbol meaning "is less than."

   tenth One out of 10 equal parts of a whole; the first place after a decimal point.

   thousandth One out of 1,000 equal parts of a whole; the third place after a decimal point.

2. Explore the new terms:
   - The words for decimal parts end in *th* or *ths*. Read aloud these numbers: 2, 0.2, 32, 0.32, 4,000, 0.004 (two, two tenths, thirty-two, thirty-two hundredths, four thousand, four thousandths). Students can practice saying whole numbers and decimals.
   - A decimal point always separates the ones and the tenths in a decimal.
   - Money can be used to explain hundredths. It takes 100 pennies to make 1 dollar. One penny is written using a decimal: $0.01 (one hundredth of a whole dollar). The symbol for money is $.
   - One penny is called 1 cent. There are 100 cents in 1 whole dollar. So 85 cents is less than 1 whole dollar and is written as $0.85 (eighty-five hundredths of 1 whole dollar).
   - For amounts less than 1 using a decimal, a 0 is written in the ones place, such as in 0.234, which is read as "two hundred thirty-four thousandths."
   - Decimal numbers are made up of two parts, the whole number part and the fractional part. The parts are separated by a decimal point.
   - The following steps are used to name decimal numbers:

     (1) Name the whole number.

     (2) Say "and" at the decimal point.

     (3) Name the fractional part in the same manner that whole numbers are named.

     (4) Say the place value of the last digit of the fractional part.

     For example: the name for 300.034 is three hundred and thirty-four thousandths.
   - Name different decimal amounts and show the value of each numeral making up the total number in a Place-Value Data table, as in the following examples:

     a. 23.45 (twenty-three and forty-five hundredths)

     b. 0.653 (six hundred fifty-three thousandths)

     c. 0.8 (eight tenths)

     d. 3,400.07 (three thousand, four hundred and seven hundredths)

PLACE-VALUE DATA

thousands	hundreds	tens	ones	decimal	tenths	hundredths	thousandths
		2	3	.	4	5	
			0	.	6	5	3
			0	.	8		
3	4	0	0	.	0	7	

- If there is a 0 in the hundredths place of a 2-digit decimal, the number can be changed to tenths, and the numbers will be equivalent. For example, fifty hundredths (0.50) equals five tenths (0.5). The symbol = is used to show that numbers or expressions have the same value. For example: 0.50 = 0.5.
- The symbol < is used to show that a number or expression is less than another. For example: 0.04 < 0.60.
- The symbol > is used to show that a number or expression is greater than another. For example: 0.60 > 0.04.

EXTENSIONS

1. *Scientific notations,* also called *power-of-10 notation,* is a way of writing any number, but is often used when writing extremely large or small numbers. A *power* is an *exponent* (a number on the right hand of and above a base number that tells how many times the base is multiplied by itself). A *base number* is a number multiplied by itself the number of times equal to the value of the exponent. In scientific notation the base is ten, and the power stands for the number of decimal places. If the power is positive, the decimal places are in front of the decimal point. So, 4×10^3 means "move the decimal point 3 places to the right and fill the empty places with zeros." Another way of saying this is to multiply by 10 three times. $4 \times 10^3 = 4 \times 10 \times 10 \times 10 = 4{,}000$.

  If the power is negative, the decimal places are behind the decimal point. So, 4×10^{-3} means "move the decimal point 3 places to the left and fill the empty places with zeros." Another way of saying this is to multiply by $^1/_{10}$ three times.
  $4 \times 10^{-3} = 4 \times {}^1/_{10} \times {}^1/_{10} \times {}^1/_{10} = 0.0004$

The usual way of writing scientific notation, called the *standard form,* is to move the decimal behind, or to the right of, the first digit greater than or equal to 1 and multiply by 10 raised to the power representing the decimal place.

EXAMPLES

A. Express 356 in scientific notation.

Think!

- Count how many places the decimal point must be moved so it is to the right of the first digit greater than or equal to 1. In the example, this is two decimal places.
- The number of places the decimal is moved is the exponent of 10. Since the decimal is moved to the left, then the exponent is positive.
- Multiply 3.56 by 10^2.

Answer: 3.56×10^2

B. Express 0.564 in scientific notation.

Think!

- Move the decimal so it is to the right of the first digit greater than or equal to 1.
- The number of places the decimal is moved is one decimal place. So 1 is the exponent of 10. Since the decimal is moved to the right, then the exponent is negative.
- Multiply 5.64 by 10^{-1}.

Answer: 5.64×10^{-1}

2. To make sure everyone gets the same answer for a problem, a set of rules known as the *order of operations* is used. The order of operations is (1) simplify inside parentheses; (2) simplify exponents; (3) multiply and divide from left to right; (4) add and subtract from left to right.

EXAMPLES

- $6 \times (3 + 2)$

  $6 \times (3 + 2) = 6 \times 5$ simplify inside parentheses first

              $= 30$ multiply

- $3^2 - 5$

  $3^2 - 5 = 9 - 5$ simplify exponents first

           $= 4$ subtract

- $8 + 6 \times 4$

  $8 + 6 \times 4 = 8 + 24$ multiply first

             $= 32$ add

- $20 \div 4 \times 6$

  $20 \div 4 \times 6 = 5 \times 6$ do left part first

             $= 30$ do right part

ANSWERS

Activity 1: Decimals

1. 0.43
2. 0.7
3. 2.55
4. five and eight hundredths
5. two and five tenths
6. one thousandth
7. twenty-three hundredths
8. ten and forty-four hundredths
9. ninety-nine hundredths
10. eight tenths

11.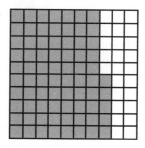

   a. zero

   b. seven

   c. seventy-five hundredths

12.

   a. two

   b. eight

   c. two and eight tenths

Activity 2: Comparing Decimals

1. **a.** 1.2   **d.** 25.60

   b. 0.30   **e.** 0.040

   c. 0.5   **f.** 0.770

2. **a.** <   **d.** >

   b. >   **e.** =

   c. <   **f.** =

Name

ACTIVITY 1

Decimals

A **decimal** is a number that uses a decimal point to show tenths, hundredths, thousandths, and so on. A **decimal point** is a dot placed between the ones place and the tenths place in decimals, such as in 2.5. A **tenth** is 1 out of 10 equal parts of a whole and is the first place after a decimal point, such as the 5 in 2.5. A **hundredth** is 1 out of 100 equal parts of a whole and is the second place after a decimal point, such as the 6 in 2.56. A **thousandth** is 1 out of 1,000 equal parts of a whole and is the third place after a decimal point, such as the 1 in 2.561.

Practice Problems

Write the name of each decimal. Then shade in the grids to show each decimal.

1. 0.4

Think!

- The grid is divided into 10 equal boxes. Each box represents one tenth of the whole grid.
- The decimal 0.4 is read as "four tenths." Thus four one-tenth boxes represent the decimal.

Answer: Four tenths

2. 1.29

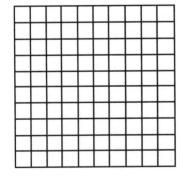
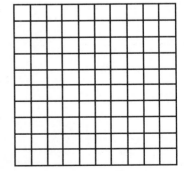

ACTIVITY 1 (continued)

Think!

- Each grid is divided into 100 boxes. Each box represents one hundredth of the whole grid.
- The decimal 1.29 is read as "one and twenty-nine hundredths." Thus 1 whole grid plus 29 boxes on a second grid represent the decimal.

Answer: One and twenty-nine hundredths

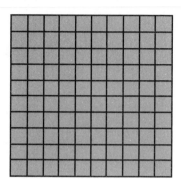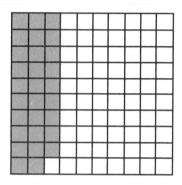

On Your Own

Write each number in decimal form.

1. forty-three hundredths _____

2. seven tenths _____

3. two and fifty-five hundredths _____

Write the name for each decimal.

4. 5.08 _____

5. 2.5 _____

6. 0.001 _____

7. 0.23 _____

8. 10.44 _____

9. 0. 99 _____

10. 0.8 _____

11. Shade in the grids to show the decimal 0.75. Then answer the questions.

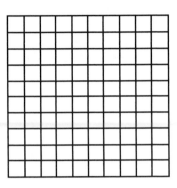

    a. How many ones? _____

    b. How many tenths? _____

    c. What is the name of the decimal? _____

12. Shade in the grids to show the decimal 2.8. Then answer the questions.

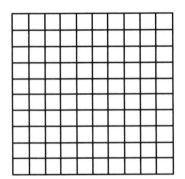 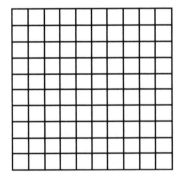 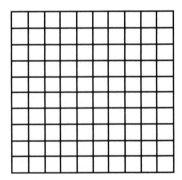

    a. How many ones? _____

    b. How many tenths? _____

    c. What is the name of the decimal?_____

Name _____

ACTIVITY 2

Comparing Decimals

Equivalent decimals are decimals that name the same amount. The symbols =, <, and > are used to compare decimals. The symbol = means "equal to." The symbol < means "is **less than**." The symbol > means "is **greater than**."

Practice Problems

1. Compare the decimals below. Use = , < , or > for each answer.

   a. 0.5 _____ 5.0

Think!

- Write the numbers with their decimal points lined up.
- Compare the digits in each place, moving from left to right.
- In comparing the digits in the ones place, 0 < 5, so 0.5 < 5.0.

$$0.5$$
$$\updownarrow \quad \updownarrow$$
$$5.0$$

Answer: 0.5 < 5.0

   b. 2.56 _____ 2.562

Think!

- Write the numbers with their decimal points lined up.
- So that each decimal has a number in the thousandths place, a 0 can be added to the right of 2.56; thus 2.560.
- Compare the digits in each place, moving from left to right.
- The digits in the ones, tenths, and hundredths place are equal. But in the thousandths place, 2 > 0. So 2.562 > 2.560.

Answer: 2.562 > 2.560

On Your Own

1. Write an equivalent decimal for each.

    a. 1.20 _____

    b. 0.3 _____

    c. 0.50 _____

    d. 25.6 _____

    e. 0.04 _____

    f. 0.77 _____

2. Write = , < , or > to compare each decimal.

    a. 0.04 _____ 0.40

    b. 22.0 _____ 0.22

    c. 0.09 _____ 9.0

    d. 6.5 _____ 0.065

    e. 0.7 _____ 0.70

    f. 3.5 _____ 3.500

Fractions

TEACHING TIPS

Benchmarks

By the end of grade 5, students should be able to
- Determine fractional parts and write fractions in lowest form.
- Use a model to represent fractional parts.
- Identify fractions in everyday situations.

By the end of grade grade 8, students should be able to
- Determine relationships between fractions.

In this chapter, students are expected to
- Count the number making up a whole and determine the fractional parts of the whole.

Preparing the Materials

Activity: Fractions
- Make a copy of the Fractions activity sheet for each student.

Investigation: Candy Parts
- Students should work in groups of three, but smaller or larger groups also will work.
- Make three copies of the Candy Parts investigation sheet for each student.
- For each group, prepare 3 resealable bags (sandwich size works well) of candy. Number the bags 1, 2, 3. Select 4 colors of candy and place varying numbers of each color in the bags. Each bag should have a different total number of candies: bag 1 should have 6 candies, bag 2 should have 12 candies, and bag 3 should have 18 candies. In each group, one Candy Parts investigation sheet will be completed for each bag. One recorder can be appointed for the group, or each student can record the results for a bag. Tell the students not to open the candy bags before or during the activity.

Presenting the Math Concepts

1. Introduce the new terms:

   circle graph A graph in the form of a circle that is divided into sections showing how the whole is broken into parts.

   data Observations and/or measured facts.

   denominator The number below the line in a fraction; the total number of equal parts in the whole.

   division bar The line separating the numerator and the denominator in a fraction.

   fraction A number used to express part of a whole and made up of two numbers separated by a line.

   graph A drawing that shows data in an organized way.

   mixed number A number made up of a whole number and a fraction.

   numerator The number above the line in a fraction; the number of equal parts being considered.

2. Explore the new terms:
   - A fraction tells how many parts a whole is broken into.
   - A fraction is made up of two numbers separated by a line called the division bar. For example, ¾ is a fraction. The top number of all fractions is called the numerator, and the bottom number is called the denominator. In this example, 3 is the numerator and 4 is the denominator.
   - A fraction is read by saying the numerator first and then the denominator. For example, ⅛ is read as "one eighth."
   - A fraction is a number that compares part of an object or set to the whole object or set. Fractions are expressed in terms of $\frac{a}{b}$ where b is not 0.
   - A fraction can be expressed as a decimal by dividing the numerator by the denominator.
   - Examples of mixed numbers are 1½ and 23⅔.
   - A circle graph is a way to show fractional parts. Graph A is broken into two equal parts so each part represents the fraction ½. Graph B is broken into four equal parts with each part representing the fraction ¼.

Circle Graphs

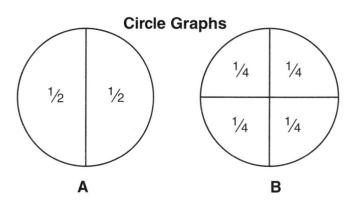

A   B

EXTENSION

1. Prepare an activity sheet with a Group Color Fraction Data table, such as the one shown here. Include questions such as the following that require students to use the data table. Note: The letters A, B, C, and D are used in the sample questions. Replace these with the colors of candy used.

   a. Compare the fractional parts of bags 1 and 2 to answer these questions:

      • List the fractional parts of the A-colored candy for the two bags in order from the greatest to the least.

      • Which bag has the greatest fractional part of C-colored candy?_____

   b. Compare the fractional parts of all three bags to answer these questions:

      • List the fractional parts of the D-colored candy for each bag in order from the greatest to the least. _____

      _____

      • List the fractional parts of the B-colored candy for each bag in order from the least to the greatest. _____

      _____

   c. Prepare a data table using decimals instead of fractions.

GROUP COLOR FRACTION DATA			
Bag	**Candy Colors**		
1			
2			
3			

ANSWERS

Activity: Fractions

1. a. $\frac{3}{5}$

   b. $\frac{2}{5}$

2. a. $\frac{3}{7}$

   b. $\frac{2}{7}$

   c. $\frac{1}{7}$

3. $1\frac{4}{8}$ or $1\frac{1}{2}$

ACTIVITY

Fractions

A **fraction** is a number used to express part of a whole and is made up of two numbers separated by a line. For example, ⅔ and ⁶⁄₁₅ are both fractions. The **division bar** is the line separating the numerator and the denominator in a fraction. The number above the line in a fraction is called the **numerator** and is the number of equal parts being considered. The number below the line in a fraction is called the **denominator** and is the total number of equal parts in the whole. A **mixed number** is a number made up of a whole number and a fraction, such as 1½. A **graph** is a drawing that shows **data** (observations and/or measured facts) in an organized way. A **circle graph** is a graph in the form of a circle that is divided into sections showing how the whole is broken into parts.

LEO THE LION

Practice Problems

1. What fractional part of the stars make up the lion's head?

Think!

- In this problem, the numerator is the number of stars in the lion's head, which is 6.
- The denominator is the total number of stars, which is 9.
- 6 of the 9 stars are in the lion's head.

Answer: ⁶⁄₉

2. What mixed number do the shaded parts of the circle graphs represent?

Think!

- One circle graph is completely shaded, thus it equals 1 whole circle.
- The second circle graph has two of the four parts shaded, thus it equals ²⁄₄ or ½.
- The mixed number representing the circle graphs is the sum of 1 + ½.

Answer: 1½

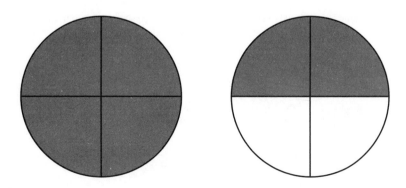

On Your Own

1. a. What fractional part of the family in the drawing are males? _____

b. What fractional part of the family are adults? _____

NUTRITIONAL NEEDS

Most —

Nutrient Amounts

Least —

Baby Boy   Girl   Boy   Woman   Man

2. a. What fractional part of the animals can fly? _____

b. What fractional part of the animals are on lily pads? _____

c. What fractional part of the animals have no legs? _____

3. What mixed number do the shaded parts of the circle graphs represent? _____

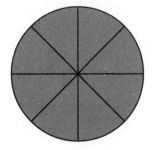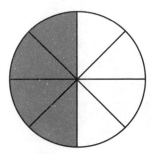

Candy Parts

PURPOSE

To determine the fractional parts of a bag of candy.

Material

plastic bag of candy

Procedure

1. Without opening the bag, look at the candy through the bag.

2. Record the different colors of candy in the first column of the Candy Fraction Data table.

3. Count the number of each candy color and record it in the data table.

4. Determine the total number of candy pieces in the bag by adding the numbers of each candy color.

5. Use the total number of candy pieces and the number of each color of candy to write the fractional part for each color in the data table.

CANDY FRACTION DATA		
Candy Color	**Number of Pieces**	**Fractional Part**

6. Use the completed data table to answer these questions:

a. Which color makes up the largest fractional part?_____

b. Which color makes up the least fractional part? _____

c. How many colors have an equal fractional part? _____

7. Select the appropriate circle graph A, B, or C and color in the sections to represent the fraction of each candy color in the candy bag.

Circle Graphs

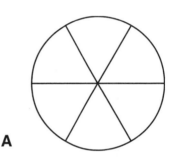

A

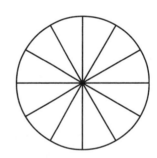

B

C

Results

Results will vary.

Percents

TEACHING TIPS

Benchmarks

By the end of grade 5, students should be able to
- Write percents as fractions and decimals, and fractions and decimals as percents.

By the end of grade 8, students should be able to
- Represent percents with fractions and decimals.

In this chapter, students are expected to
- Convert numbers among percents, decimals, and fractions.

Preparing the Materials

Activity 1: Connecting Percents, Fractions, and Decimals
- Make a copy of the Connecting Percents, Fractions, and Decimals activity sheet for each student.

Activity 2: Percent of a Number
- Make a copy of the Percent of a Number activity sheet for each student.

Presenting the Math Concepts

1. Introduce the new term:

   percent (%) Per hundred. A way to compare a number to 100.

2. Explore the new term:
   - Percent is a way to compare a number to 100.
   - The percent symbol, %, means hundredths. So 60% is read as "sixty percent" and means $^{60}/_{100}$ or sixty hundredths.
   - Percent numbers can be expressed as a decimal number by first expressing the percent as a fraction, then dividing the numerator by the denominator, which is 100. For example, $60\% = {^{60}/_{100}} = 0.6$.
   - Percent used to be written as a fraction with the numerator over 100. Over time, the bar of the fraction and the 100 were combined to become the % symbol used today.
   - Information on a circle graph is usually shown as a percentage or fraction. The larger the area of the graph used, the greater the percentage represented.
   - The whole circle of a circle graph represents 100% or the total amount.

- A circle graph is often called a pie chart because when divided into sections each section looks like a piece of pie.

EXTENSION

Bags of different-colored candy pieces can be used to study the percent of different colors of candy in each bag. Have students count the number of candies of each color in their bags and use that number and the total number of candies in the bag to come up with percentages of each color in the bag. You may wish to have extra candy that is not part of the investigation for eating.

ANSWERS

Activity 1: Connecting Percents, Fractions, and Decimals

1. **a.** 35%
   b. 0.2%

2. **a.** 0.68
   b. 0.72

3. **a.** 50%
   b. 50%
   c. 75%
   d. 25%

Activity 2: Percent of a Number

1. **a.** 24
   b. 4.5
   c. 2.5

2. **a.** 7.5
   b. 100
   c. 225

3. **a.** 3
   b. 12
   c. 9
   d. 6

Connecting Percents, Fractions, and Decimals

Percent (%) means per hundred. Percent is a way to compare a number to 100. A fraction is a number used to express part of a whole. A decimal is a number that uses a decimal point to show tenths, hundredths, thousandths, and so on.

To change a percent to a decimal, divide the number by 100. To change a decimal to a percent, multiply the number by 100. To change a fraction to a percent, first divide the numerator by the denominator, then multiply by 100.

Practice Problems

1. Change 45% to a decimal.

Think!
- To change a percent to a decimal, divide the number by 100.

  $45 \div 100 = ?$

Answer: 0.45

2. Change 0.25 to a percent.

Think!
- To change a decimal to a percent, multiply the number by 100.

  $0.25 \times 100 = ?$

Answer: 25%

3. Change $\frac{1}{5}$ to a percent.

Think!
- To change a fraction to a percent, first divide the numerator by the denominator.

  $1 \div 5 = 0.20$

- Then multiply by 100.

  $0.20 \times 100 = ?$

Answer: 20%

On Your Own

1. Change these decimals to percents:

    a. 0.35 _____   **b.** 0.002 _____

2. Change these percents to decimals:

    a. 68% _____   **b.** 72% _____

3. Change these fractions to percents:

    a. $\frac{1}{2}$ _____   **c.** $\frac{3}{4}$ _____

    b. $\frac{2}{4}$ _____   **d.** $\frac{25}{100}$ _____

Percent of a Number

To find the percent of any number, you can use one of two methods:

Method 1: Use a Fraction

- Express the percent as a fraction per 100.

- Multiply the fraction times the number.

- Divide the numerator by the denominator.

Method 2: Use a Decimal

- Express the percent as a decimal.

- Multiply the decimal times the number.

Practice Problem

Find 12% of 20.

Think!

Method 1: Use a Fraction

- Express the percent as a fraction per 100: $12\% = \frac{12}{100}$.

- Multiply the fraction times the number: $\frac{12}{100} \times 20 = \frac{240}{100}$.

- Divide the numerator by the denominator: $240 \div 100 = ?$

Answer: 2.4

Method 2: Use a Decimal

- Express the percent as a decimal: $12\% = \frac{12}{100} = 0.12$.

- Multiply the decimal times the number: $0.12 \times 20 = ?$

Answer: 2.4

On Your Own

1. Find the indicated percent of each number using Method 1.

   a. 60% of 40 _____

   b. 30% of 15 _____

   c. 5% of 50 _____

© 2005 by John Wiley & Sons, Inc.

ACTIVITY 2 (continued)

2. Find the indicated percent of each number using Method 2.

    a. 15% of 50 _____

    b. 50% of 200 _____

    c. 75% of 300 _____

3. The circle graph below shows the percentage of different hair colors in a class of 30 students. Use the graph to determine how many students have each hair color.

    a. Red _____

    b. Brown _____

    c. Blond _____

    d. Black _____

Ratios

TEACHING TIPS

Benchmarks

By the end of grade 5, students should be able to
• Use ratios to describe relationships mathematically.

By the end of grade 8, students should be able to
• Represent ratios with models.

In this chapter, students are expected to
• Write ratios in three different ways.

Preparing the Materials

Investigation 1: Red to White
• Make a copy of the Red to White investigation sheet for each student.
• Prepare 1 bag of beans for each pair of students. Place 10 red beans and 10 white beans in each bag.

Investigation 2: Color Ratio
• Make a copy of the Color Ratio investigation sheet for each student.
• Prepare colored water by adding 10 drops of food coloring to 1 cup (250 mL) of tap water.
• Provide a bag of blue and a bag of yellow water for each pair of students. Place about ¼ cup (63 mL) of colored water in each quart-size (liter-size) resealable bag.

Presenting the Math Concepts

1. Introduce the new term:

   ratio A pair of numbers used to compare quantities.

2. Explore the new term:
   • A ratio can be expressed in three different ways: (1) in words, (2) with a colon, or (3) as a fraction. For example, in comparing the number of your eyes to the number of your toes, the ratio could look like this:

Comparison	In words, using "to"	With a colon	As a fraction
Eyes to toes	2 to 10	2:10	²⁄₁₀

   • A ratio is generally written as a simplified fraction; for the comparison of eyes to toes, the ratio would be 1 to 5, 1:5, or ⅕.
   • A ratio is not written as a mixed number (a number containing a whole number and a fraction).
   • Order is important when writing a ratio. For the eyes-to-toes comparison, the ratio is 1 to 5, not 5 to 1.
   • A ratio can compare a part to a part (P/P), a part to a whole (P/W), or a whole to a part (W/P).

EXTENSION

Redo the Color Ratio investigation, this time adding a bag of red water for each group. Allow students to create their own Ratio Data tables. Ratios of two colors as well as ratios of three colors can be used.

Red to White

PURPOSE

To determine the ratio of objects.

Materials

1 bag of 10 red and 10 white beans
pencil
red crayon

Procedure

1. Without looking, scoop out a small handful of beans from the bag.

2. Make a drawing of the beans on the Bean Ratio Data table. Use the crayon to color the red beans.

BEAN RATIO DATA			
Drawing			
Comparison of Beans	**Simplified Ratio**		
	In words, using "to"	**With a colon**	**As a fraction**
red to white			
white to red			
red to whole			
white to whole			
whole to red			
whole to white			

3. Write the ratio of the beans in the data table in the ways indicated. "Red" is for all the red beans, "white" is for all of the white beans, and "whole" is for total number of beans scooped out of the bag.

Results

Results will vary depending on how many beans you pick. For example, if 3 red beans and 4 white beans are scooped out of the bag, the table would look like this:

BEAN RATIO DATA			
Comparison of Beans	**Simplified Ratio**		
	In words, using "to"	**With a colon**	**As a fraction**
red to white	3 to 4	3:4	¾
white to red	4 to 3	4:3	4⁄3
red to whole	3 to 7	3:7	3⁄7
white to whole	4 to 7	4:7	4⁄7
whole to red	7 to 3	7:3	7⁄3
whole to white	7 to 4	7:4	7⁄4

Why?

A **ratio** is a pair of numbers used to compare quantities. It is expressed in words using the word "to," with a colon, or as a fraction. A ratio compares a part to a part (P/P), a part to a whole (P/W), or a whole to a part (W/P). In this activity, the parts are red beans and white beans. The whole is the sum of red and white beans.

Color Ratio

PURPOSE

To determine the colors produced in mixtures made from different ratios of colors.

Materials

marker
3 sandwich-size resealable plastic bags
two 1-teaspoon (5-mL) measuring
   spoons
2 bags of colored water, yellow and
   blue
helper

Procedure

1. Use the marker to label the empty plastic bags A, B, and C.

2. Look at the Color Ratio Data table below. Write the ratio for each mixture on the label of the bag indicated.

3. Prepare each mixture by asking your helper to hold open the bags of colored water one at a time while you dip out a measured amount. For example, the mixture in bag A will be a combination of 1 teaspoon of blue water and 1 teaspoon of yellow water. (Use a different measuring spoon for each color of water.)

4. Seal bag A, then gently shake it.

5. Repeat steps 3 and 4 to prepare mixtures B and C.

6. Hold the three bags up to a light and compare their colors. Write a description of the colors in bags A, B, and C in the Resulting Color column of the data table.

Results

The combination of different ratios of blue and yellow water produced various shades of green.

Why?

Colored materials have *colorants* (chemical substances that give color to materials). Colorants that dissolve in liquids are called *dyes*. When two different colorants are mixed, a third color is produced. For example, when blue water is mixed with yellow water, the resulting mixture appears green. The ratio of the parts produces different shades of green. The more yellow in the mixture, the lighter the green shade.

COLOR RATIO DATA			
Mixture	**Ratio**	**Combination**	**Resulting Color**
A blue to yellow	1:1	blue—1 spoon yellow—1 spoon	
B blue to yellow	2:1	blue—2 spoons yellow—1 spoon	
C yellow to blue	2:1	yellow—2 spoons blue—1 spoon	

Algebra

Algebra is the branch of mathematics in which arithmetic relations are explored using signs and letters to represent numbers. Algebra is a key to problem-solving. Problem solving is the application of mathematical concepts in new situations. As in arithmetic, the basic operations of algebra are addition, subtraction, multiplication, and division. While arithmetic can produce only specific examples, algebra can generalize mathematical relationships. For example, the equation $3^2 = 3 \times 3$ is true only for the number 3. But the algebraic equation $a^2 = a \times a$ is true for any number, and it means that the square of any number equals that number multiplied by itself. In this section, some of the basic tools of algebra—algebraic expression, equations, and formulas—will be studied and used to solve problems related to everyday situations.

Algebraic Expressions

TEACHING TIPS

Benchmarks

By the end of grade 5, students should be able to
- Understand the difference between a variable and a constant.
- Evaluate expressions.
- Use tables and symbols to represent and describe relationships.

By the end of grade 8, students should be able to
- Understand and use the associative, commutative, and distributive properties.
- Select and use appropriate operations to solve problems.

In this chapter, students are expected to
- Substitute values for variables.
- Compare constants and variables.
- Use the order of operations to find the values of expressions.

Preparing the Materials

Activity 1: Quantities, Constants, and Variables
- Make a copy of the Quantities, Constants, and Variables activity sheet for each student.

Activity 2: Algebraic Expressions
- Make a copy of the Algebraic Expressions activity sheet for each student.

Presenting the Math Concepts

1. Introduce the new terms:

   algebraic expression A combination of constants and variables and one or more operational symbols.

   base number In reference to an exponent, it is a number multiplied by itself the number of times equal to the value of the exponent.

   constant A quantity whose value does not change.

   exponent A number to the right and above a base number that tells how many times the base number is multiplied by itself.

   quantity An amount or anything that can be measured by a number.

   substituting Replacing a variable with a known value.

   variable A quantity whose value changes. A letter is often used to represent a variable.

2. Explore the new terms:
   - Algebra is the branch of mathematics in which arithmetic relations are explored using operational symbols $(+, -, \times, \div)$ and letters to represent numbers.
   - A quantity is anything that can be measured by a number.
   - A quantity whose value does not change is a constant. An example is the number of ounces in a pound, which is always 16.
   - A quantity whose value *does* change is a variable. An example is air temperature, which changes frequently.
   - A letter is used to represent a variable, and the letters used often remind you of what they represent. For example, the letters s, d, and t can be used to represent speed, distance, and time, respectively. Variables are often set in italic type to avoid confusion.
   - Calculator keys use variables to represent the number shown in the display. For example, the x^2 key will square the number in the display. Squaring a number means multiplying the number by itself. For example, $5^2 = 5 \times 5 = 25$.
   - An expression combines numbers with one or more operations, such as $3 + 2$, 3×4, and $4 \times 5 - 6 + 9$.
   - An expression that contains a variable, such as $3 + n$, is called an algebraic expression.
   - An algebraic expression can be evaluated by replacing the variable with a known value. This is known as substituting a value for the variable.
   - There are many ways to indicate multiplication of a variable. For example, 4 times y can be written $4 \times y$, $4 \cdot y$, $4(y)$, or $4y$.
   - The repeated multiplication of the same number can be represented by an exponent. The base number is the number to be multiplied. The exponent is the number that tells how many times the base is multiplied by itself. In the number 2^3, 2 is the base and 3 is the exponent. Numbers involving exponents can be written in three forms:

     Exponential notation: 2^3

     Expanded form: $2 \times 2 \times 2$

     Standard form: 8

EXTENSIONS

1. What expressions would generate the given evaluations?

x	?	?	?	?	?
3	18	12	9	15	30
5	20	10	25	25	18

Answers: $x + 15$, $15 - x$, x^2, $5x$, $\frac{90}{x}$

2. A *coefficient* is any factor of an expression or any product of factors of an expression. For example, the expression $5xy$ can be written indicating the different coefficient of a quantity expressed in parentheses:

a. 5 is the coefficient of xy $5(xy)$

b. x is the coefficient of $5y$ $x(5y)$

c. y is the coefficient $5x$ $y(5x)$

d. xy is the coefficient of 5 $xy(5)$

e. $5y$ is the coefficient of x $5y(x)$

f. $5x$ is the coefficient of y $5x(y)$

Students can rewrite expressions, such as $6ab$ and $8cd$, indicating the different coefficients.

ANSWERS

Activity 1: Quantities, Constants, and Variables

1. constant
2. variable
3. variable
4. variable
5. constant
6. variable
7. constant
8. variable
9. variable
10. constant

Activity 2: Algebraic Expressions

1.

x	x + 8	x(8)	$\frac{12}{x}$	x^2	48 − x
2	$2 + 8 = 10$	$2(8) = 16$	$\frac{12}{2} = 12 \div 2 = 6$	$2^2 = 2 \times 2 = 4$	$48 - 2 = 46$
3	$3 + 8 = 11$	$3(8) = 24$	$\frac{12}{3} = 12 \div 3 = 4$	$3^2 = 3 \times 3 = 9$	$48 - 3 = 45$
4	$4 + 8 = 12$	$4(8) = 32$	$\frac{12}{4} = 12 \div 4 = 3$	$4^2 = 4 \times 4 = 16$	$48 - 4 = 44$

2.

x	32 + x	x(4)	$\frac{30}{x}$	x^2	50 − x
3	$32 + 3 = 35$	$3(4) = 12$	$\frac{30}{3} = 30 \div 3 = 10$	$3^2 = 3 \times 3 = 9$	$50 - 3 = 47$
5	$32 + 5 = 37$	$5(4) = 20$	$\frac{30}{5} = 30 \div 5 = 6$	$5^2 = 5 \times 5 = 25$	$50 - 5 = 45$
10	$32 + 10 = 42$	$10(4) = 40$	$\frac{30}{10} = 30 \div 10 = 3$	$10^2 = 10 \times 10 = 100$	$50 - 10 = 40$

3. **a.** $180x$, where x is the speed of a giant tortoise.

b. $x + 43$, where x is the top speed of a human in miles per hour.

c. $\frac{x}{2}$, where x is the flying speed of a canvasback duck.

d. $x - 14$, where x is the speed of a red fox in miles per hour.

Quantities, Constants, and Variables

A **quantity** is an amount or anything that can be measured by a number. A quantity whose value does not change is a **constant**. A quantity whose value changes is a **variable.**

Practice Problems

Identify each as a variable or a constant.

    a. The number of eyes on dogs.

Think!

- Dogs always have two eyes.
- A constant is a quantity whose value does not change.

Answer: constant

    b. The length of a bedroom.

Think!

- The length of a bedroom can be different, so this number can change.
- A variable is a quantity whose value changes.

Answer: variable

On Your Own

Identify each as a variable or a constant.

  1. The number of legs on an insect. _____

  2. The time it takes to run a mile. _____

  3. The number of pages in a book. _____

  4. The weight of a kitten. _____

  5. The number of inches in 1 foot. _____

  6. The number of times a hummingbird's wings beat in one minute. _____

  7. The number of minutes in an hour. _____

  8. The price of a CD. _____

  9. The length of a movie. _____

10. The number of legs on a bird. _____

8

ACTIVITY 2

Algebraic Expressions

An **algebraic expression** is a combination of constants and variables and one or more operational symbols. Letters are used to represent variables in algebraic expressions. **Substituting** means replacing a variable with a known value. A **base number** is a number multiplied by itself the number of times equal to the value of the exponent. An **exponent** is a number to the right of and above a base number that tells how many times the base is multiplied by itself.

Practice Problems

1. Evaluate the expression for $x = 1, 2, 3$.

a. $9x$

Think!

$9x$ means "9 times x." To evaluate the expression, a value must be substituted for the variable, which is x.

Answer:

x	$9x$
1	$9 \times 1 = 9$
2	$9 \times 2 = 18$
3	$9 \times 3 = 27$

b. $18/x$

Think!

$18/x$ means "18 divided by x." To evaluate the expression, substitute the given values for x.

Answer:

x	$18/x$
1	$18/1 = 18 \div 1 = 18$
2	$18/2 = 18 \div 2 = 9$
3	$18/3 = 18 \div 3 = 6$

c. x^2

Think!

The number x^2 means "the base number, x, multiplied by itself 2 times." To evaluate the expression, substitute the given values for x.

Answer:

x	x^2
1	$1 \times 1 = 1$
2	$2 \times 2 = 4$
3	$3 \times 3 = 9$

ACTIVITY 2 (continued)

2. Write as an expression.

A monkey can lift 50 times its own weight (w). How many pounds can a monkey lift?

Think!

• Times means multiplication.

Answer: 50w

On Your Own

1. Complete the table by evaluating each expression for $x = 2, 3, 4$.

x	$x + 8$	$x(8)$	$^{12}/x$	x^2	$48 - x$
2					
3					
4					

2. Complete the table by evaluating each expression for $x = 3, 5, 10$.

x	$32 + x$	$x(4)$	$^{30}/x$	x^2	$50 - x$
3					
5					
10					

3. Write as an expression. Use x for the variable.

a. A jackrabbit can run 180 times as fast as a giant tortoise. How fast can a jackrabbit run? _____

b. A cheetah runs 43 miles per hour faster than the top speed for a human. How fast does a cheetah run? _____

c. An ostrich can run about half as fast as a canvasback duck can fly. How fast can an ostrich run? _____

d. A mamba snake crawls on its belly at a speed 14 miles per hour slower than a red fox. How fast can a mamba snake crawl? _____

Algebraic Equations

TEACHING TIPS

Benchmarks

By the end of grade 5, students should be able to
- Use equations to show relationships between expressions.
- Substitute values for variables.
- Use inverse operations.

By the end of grade 8, students should be able to
- Select and use appropriate operations to solve problems.

In this chapter, students are expected to
- Determine if an equation is true or false.
- Solve equations using inverse operations.

Preparing the Materials

Activity 1: Substituting
- Make a copy of the Substituting activity sheet for each student.

Activity 2: Solving Addition and Subtraction Equations
- Make a copy of the Solving Addition and Subtraction Equations activity sheet for each student.

Activity 3: Solving Multiplication and Division Equations
- Make a copy of the Solving Multiplication and Division Equations activity sheet for each student.

Presenting the Math Concepts

1. Introduce the new terms:

   algebraic equation An equation with a variable.

   solution of an algebraic equation The value of the variable that makes the equation true.

   solve To find the solution of an equation.

   unequal sign ($\neq$) A sign used to show that two expressions are not equal.

2. Explore the new terms:
   - An equation with a variable is true or false depending on the value of the variable. For example, if $x = 3$ is substituted into these equations:

     a. $x + 4 = 7$ is true, because $3 + 4 = 7$

     b. $x - 2 = 4$ is false, because $3 - 2 \neq 4$
   - Inverse operations undo each other. For example, addition and subtraction undo each other and multiplication and division undo each other.

- When you change one side of an equation, you must change the other side in the same way so that the equation remains equal.

- To solve an equation, you must undo what was done to the variable. For example, in the equation $x + 2 = 5$, the variable has 2 added to it. To undo adding 2 to the variable, subtract 2 from both sides.

$$
\begin{aligned}
x + 2 &= 5 && \text{original equation} \\
x + 2 - \mathbf{2} &= 5 - \mathbf{2} && \text{subtract 2 from both sides} \\
x + 0 &= 3 \\
x &= 3
\end{aligned}
$$

Check the answer by substituting the value in the original equation:

$$
\begin{aligned}
x + 2 &= 5 \\
\mathbf{3} + 2 &= 5
\end{aligned}
$$

In the equation $x - 3 = 8$, the variable has 3 subtracted from it. To undo subtracting 3 from the variable, add 3 to both sides.

$$
\begin{aligned}
x - 3 &= 8 && \text{original equation} \\
x - 3 + \mathbf{3} &= 8 + \mathbf{3} && \text{add 3 to both sides} \\
x - 0 &= 11 \\
x &= 11
\end{aligned}
$$

Check the answer by substituting the value in the original equation:

$$
\begin{aligned}
x - 3 &= 8 \\
\mathbf{11} - 3 &= 8
\end{aligned}
$$

In the equation $2x = 8$, the variable is multiplied by 2. To undo multiplying the variable by 2, divide both sides by 2. Express the division as a fraction.

$$
\begin{aligned}
2x &= 8 && \text{original equation} \\
\tfrac{2x}{2} &= \tfrac{8}{2} && \text{divide both sides by 2} \\
x &= 4
\end{aligned}
$$

Check the answer by substituting the value in the original equation:

$$
\begin{aligned}
2x &= 8 \\
2 \times \mathbf{4} &= 8
\end{aligned}
$$

In the equation $x \div 4 = 7$, the variable is divided by 4. To undo dividing the variable by 4, multiply both sides by 4. (Note: Expressing $x \div 4$ as a fraction makes it easier to see how the multiple of 4 is cancelled.)

$$
\begin{aligned}
\tfrac{x}{4} &= 7 && \text{original equation} \\
\tfrac{x}{4} \cdot \mathbf{4} &= 7 \cdot \mathbf{4} && \text{multiply both sides by 4} \\
\tfrac{4x}{4} &= 28 \\
x &= 28
\end{aligned}
$$

Check the answer by substituting the value in the original equation:

$$x/4 = 7$$
$$28/4 = 7$$

- You solve the equation the same way whether the variable is on the left or the right side of the equal sign. For example, solve for x in the equation $30 = x + 2$.

$$30 = x + 2 \quad \text{original equation}$$
$$30 - 2 = x + 2 - 2 \quad \text{subtract 2 from both sides}$$
$$28 = x$$

or

$$x = 28$$

EXTENSION

1. Students can solve equations that include multiple operations, such as $3x + 5 = 20$. For this problem, the solution would be in two steps:

(a)
$$3x + 5 = 20 \quad \text{original equation}$$
$$3x + 5 - 5 = 20 - 5 \quad \text{subtract 5 from each side}$$
$$3x = 15$$

(b)
$$3x = 15 \quad \text{original equation}$$
$$3x/3 = 15/3 \quad \text{divide both sides by 3}$$
$$x = 5$$

Check: $3x + 5 = 20$
$$3 \cdot 5 + 5 = 20$$
$$15 + 5 = 20$$

Sample Equations

1. $4x - 5 = 15$ ($x = 5$)
2. $35 - 5x = 25$ ($x = 2$)
3. $25 + x/6 = 55$ ($x = 180$)

ANSWERS

Activity 1: Substituting

1. false
2. true
3. true
4. false
5. true
6. false
7. true
8. true
9. false
10. true

Activity 2: Solving Addition and Subtraction Equations

1. $R = 17$
2. $F = 250$
3. $H = 118$
4. $A = 78$
5. $B = 30$
6. $P = 1,690$

Activity 3: Solving Multiplication and Division Equations

1. $x = 100$
2. $z = 5$
3. $x = 8$
4. $b = 32$
5. $G = 8$
6. $W = 363$

ACTIVITY 1

Substituting

An equation is a statement that uses an equal sign (=) to show that two expressions are equal. An **unequal sign (≠)** is used to show that two expressions are not equal. An **algebraic equation** is an equation with a variable, which can be true or false depending on the value of the variable. Replacing a variable with a known value is called substituting.

Practice Problem

Is the equation true or false for the given value of the variable?

$18 + x = 24, x = 6$

Think!

- Substitute the value of x in the equation:

    $18 + 6 = 24$

- Does $18 + 6$ equal 24? Yes.

- Is the equation true or false?

Answer: true

On Your Own

Is the equation true or false for the given value of the variable?

1. $2 + N = 8, N = 5$ _____

2. $3x = 15, x = 5$ _____

3. $32 - x = 22, x = 10$ _____

4. $25 \div z = 6, z = 5$ _____

5. $1R = 2, R = 2$ _____

6. $Y/3 = 13, Y = 12$ _____

7. $0/P = 0, P = 9$ _____

8. $32B \div 2 = 32, B = 2$ _____

9. $S + 35 = 60, S = 24$ _____

10. $3 \times 3M = 18, M = 2$ _____

ACTIVITY 2

Solving Addition and Subtraction Equations

You **solve** an algebraic equation by finding the solution, which is the value of the variable. The value of the variable that makes the equation true is called the **solution of an algebraic equation**. Inverse operations, such as addition and subtraction, undo each other. You can use inverse operations to solve some addition and subtraction problems.

Practice Problems

Solve the equations using inverse operations. Check each answer.

a. $x + 6 = 10$

Think!

- When changing one side of an equation, to keep it equal you must make the same change to the other side.
- To undo adding 6 to the variable, subtract 6 from both sides.

$$x + 6 = 10 \qquad \text{original equation}$$
$$x + 6 - \mathbf{6} = 10 - \mathbf{6} \qquad \text{subtract 6 from both sides}$$
$$x + 0 = 4$$
$$x = 4$$

Check the answer by substituting the value in the original equation:

$$x + 6 = 10$$
$$\mathbf{4} + 6 = 10$$

Answer: $x = 4$

b. $x - 10 = 35$

Think!

- To undo subtracting 10 from the variable, add 10 to both sides.

$$x - 10 = 35 \qquad \text{original equation}$$
$$x - 10 + \mathbf{10} = 35 + \mathbf{10} \qquad \text{add 10 to both sides}$$
$$x + 0 = 45$$
$$x = 45$$

Check the answer by substituting the value in the original equation:

$$x - 10 = 35$$
$$\mathbf{45} - 10 = 35$$

Answer: $x = 45$

On Your Own

Solve the equations using inverse operations. Check each answer.

1. $R + 75 = 92$

    Check: _____

    Answer: _____

2. $230 + F = 480$

    Check: _____

    Answer: _____

3. $H - 95 = 23$

    Check: _____

    Answer: _____

4. $58 = A - 20$

    Check: _____

    Answer: _____

5. $65 = 35 + B$

    Check: _____

    Answer: _____

6. $940 = P - 750$

    Check: _____

    Answer: _____

Solving Multiplication and Division Equations

You can use inverse operations to solve multiplication and division problems. Just remember that inverse operations, such as multiplication and division, undo each other.

Practice Problems

Solve the equations using inverse operations. Check each answer.

a. $3x = 15$

Think!

- To undo multiplying the variable by 3, divide both sides by 3. Express the division as a fraction:

$$3x = 15 \qquad \text{original equation}$$
$$\tfrac{3x}{3} = \tfrac{15}{3} \qquad \text{divide both sides by 3}$$
$$x = \mathbf{5}$$

Check the answer by substituting the value in the original equation:

$$3x = 15$$
$$3 \cdot 5 = 15$$

Answer: $x = 5$

b. $x \div 5 = 6$

Think!

- To undo dividing the variable by 5, first express $x \div 5$ as a fraction, then multiply both sides by 5.

$$\tfrac{x}{5} = 6 \qquad \text{original equation}$$
$$\tfrac{x}{5} \cdot 5 = 6 \cdot 5 \qquad \text{multiply both sides by 5}$$
$$\tfrac{5x}{5} = 30$$
$$x = 30$$

Check the answer by substituting the value in the original equation:

$$x \div 5 = 6$$
$$\tfrac{30}{5} = 6$$

Answer: $x = 30$

On Your Own

Solve the equations using inverse operations. Check each answer.

1. $x \div 5 = 20$

Check: _____

Answer: _____

2. $6z = 30$

Check: _____

Answer: _____

3. $72 = 9x$

Check: _____

Answer: _____

4. $b \div 8 = 4$

Check: _____

Answer: _____

5. $8G = 64$

Check: _____

Answer: _____

6. $W/11 = 33$

Check: _____

Answer: _____

Formulas

TEACHING TIPS

Benchmarks

By the end of grade 5, students should be able to
- Use formulas to describe relationships between two sets of related data.
- Substitute values for variables.

By the end of grade 8, students should be able to
- Select and use appropriate operations to solve problems.

In this chapter, students are expected to
- Use formulas to show relationships between or among quantities.
- Use variables to represent quantities.

Preparing the Materials

Activity: Formulas
- Make a copy of the Formulas activity sheet for each student.

Investigation: Jumpers
- Make a copy of the Jumpers investigation sheet for each student. You'll need 2 feet (0.6 m) of string for each group.

Presenting the Math Concepts

1. Introduce the new term:

   formula A rule represented by an equation that shows relationships between or among quantities.

2. Explore the new term:
   - A formula contains one or more variables. For example, the formula for finding the speed of a moving object is $s = \frac{d}{t}$. The formula is read as "speed (s) equals distance (d) divided by time (t)."

- To find the value of one variable in a formula, the value of all the other variables in the formula must be known. Replacing variables with values is called substituting. For example, to find the value of speed in the formula $s = \frac{d}{t}$, the value of distance (d) and time (t) must be substituted. If 20 miles is substituted for d and 2 hours is substituted for t, then the value for s would be:

$$s = \frac{d}{t}$$
$$s = 20 \text{ mi}/2 \text{ hr}$$
$$s = 10 \text{ mi}/1 \text{ hr}$$

EXTENSION

Students can use the formula $b = \frac{m}{h}$ to determine their body mass index (BMI). In the formula, m is mass measured in kilograms, and h is height measured in meters. Note: If necessary, use the formula $m = \frac{p}{2.2}$ to convert pounds (p) to kilograms, and $h = 0.025x$ to convert inches (x) to meters.

ANSWERS

Activity: Formulas

1. 3 sec
2. **a.** 50 km/sec
   b. 125 mi/hr
3. **a.** 3.5 gal
   b. 80 cups
4. **a.** 230 mi/hr
   b. 125 km/hr
5. 12 in

Formulas

A **formula** is a rule represented by an equation that shows relationships between or among quantities. To find the value of one variable in a formula, the value of all the other variables in the formula must be known. Replacing variables with values is called substituting.

Practice Problems

1. The formula $f = x/12$ is used to change inches (x) to feet (f). Find out how many feet are equal to 36 inches.

Think!

- Substitute the value of x in the formula:

$f = x/12$	original formula
$f = 36/12$	substitute 36 for x
$f = 3$	divide

Answer: 3 ft

2. The formula for speed is $s = d/t$. Substitute the given values into the formula and calculate the distance.

Thunder was heard 3 seconds (t) after a flash of lightning was seen. If sound travels at a speed of about 0.2 mile per second (s) in air, how far away (d) was the lightning?

Think!

- The formula for speed is $s = d/t$. To solve for d in the formula, the variable d must be isolated. Since d is divided by t, to undo dividing the variable by t, multiply the formula on both sides of the equal sign by t.

$s = d/t$	original formula
$s \times t = d/t \times t$	multiply both sides by t
$s \times t = d$	

- Substitute in the values for s and t and calculate for d.

  $$s \times t = d$$
  $$0.2 \text{ mi/sec} \times 3 \text{ sec} = 0.6 \text{ mi}$$

Answer: 0.6 mi

On Your Own

1. The formula for speed is $s = \frac{d}{t}$. Substitute the given values into the formula and calculate the distance. Sound travels through steel at a speed of 5,000 meters per second. How long will it take the sound of a train moving along steel railroad tracks to be heard if the train is at a distance of 15,000 m?

Answer: _____

2. The formula for speed is $s = \frac{d}{t}$. Substitute the values for d and t into the formula. Then use the formula to find s.

   a. $d = 150$ km, $t = 3$ sec

   $s =$ _____

   b. $d = 250$ m, $t = 2$ hr

   $s =$ _____

3. Use the formula $g = \frac{c}{16}$ to convert cups (c) to gallons (g).

   a. How many gallons equal 56 cups?

   Answer: _____

   b. 5 gallons equal how many cups?

   Answer: _____

4. The formula $g = a - w$ is used to determine ground speed of an airplane. Substitute the values for a (airspeed of aircraft) and w (head-on wind speed) into the formula. Then use the formula to find g (ground speed of the aircraft).

   a. $a = 350$ mi/hr; $w = 120$ mi/hr

   $g =$ _____

   b. $a = 150$ km/hr; $w = 25$ km/hr

   $g =$ _____

5. The formula $i = \frac{c}{2.5}$ can be used to convert centimeters (c) to inches (i). How many inches are equal to 30 cm?

   Answer: _____

Jumpers

PURPOSE
To use a formula to determine how many times your length you can jump and how far you can jump if you were another animal.

Materials
yardstick (meterstick) or
   measuring tape
scissors
string
pencil
helper

Procedure

1. Measure and cut two 2-ft (0.6-m) pieces of string.

2. Lay the strings on the ground in an open area so they are 12 ft (3.6 m) apart. One string will be the starting line and the other the jumping line.

3. Stand on the starting line and run toward the jumping line. When you reach the jumping line, jump forward as far as possible.

4. Ask your helper to place the pencil on the ground where you land.

5. Write your name in the Jumping Data table.

6. Using the yardstick (meterstick), measure from the jumping line to the pencil marking where you land. Record this jumping distance (d) in the table. (Note: Use inch (in) for English measurements and centimeter (cm) for metric measurements.)

7. Measure your height in inches using the same measurement unit used in step 6. Record this as the length of body (L) in the table.

8. Using the formula $t = d/L$, find how many times your body length (t) you can jump. Record this in the table.

JUMPING DATA			
Name	Jumping distance, d	Body length, L (Height)	How many times body, length, $t = d/L$

9. Some animals can jump many times their body length, as shown in the data table. Using the formula $d = t \times L$ where L is your height (use inches or cm), find out how far you could leap if you could jump as well as the different animals.

Animal	How many times body length, t	Body length, L (Height)	Jumping distance, $d = t \times L$
Gray kangaroo	8		
Goliath frog	20		
Kangaroo rat	48		
Flea	200		

Results

You have used a formula to determine how many times your body length you can jump as well as how far you could jump if you jumped as well as different animals.

Why?

Using this formula $t = d/L$, you substituted values for d (distance jumped) and L (your body length) to find t (how many times your body length you can jump). Using the formula $d = t \times L$, you substituted values for t (how many times their own body length a specific animal could jump) and L (your body length) to find d (how far you could jump if you jumped as far as that animal). You discovered how far you could jump if you jumped as far as a gray kangaroo, a goliath frog, a kangaroo rat, and a flea.

Measurements

Measure and measurement are terms that describe the process of finding the amount of something, including its size, volume, length, mass, weight, and temperature. The use of measurement tools such as a ruler, scale, or thermometer is one of the most important mathematical skills, and the best way to develop this skill is by hands-on experience.

The **English system** is a system of measurements based on the units foot, pound, pint, and second. The **metric system** is a decimal system of measurements based on the units meter (m), gram (g), liter (L), and second. In this book both the English and metric systems of measurement are used. The term *metric system* is used instead of the *SI system,* which is the internationally agreed-upon method of using the metric system of measurement. Students need to know how to convert different units of measurement within each system as well as between the two systems.

Conversions

11

TEACHING TIPS

Benchmarks

By the end of grade 5, students should be able to
- Describe numerical relationships between units of measure within the same measurement system, such as 1 centimeter equals 10 millimeters.
- Describe numerical relationships between units of measure between two different measurement systems, such as 1 pound equals 454 grams.

By the end of grade 8, students should be able to
- Convert measures within the same measurement system and between different measurement systems based on relationships between units.

In this chapter, students are expected to
- Use conversion factors to convert numbers from a metric unit to an English unit.
- Use conversion factors to convert numbers from one metric unit to another.
- Use a metric unit line to convert numbers from one metric unit to another.

Preparing the Materials

Activity 1: Metric Conversions
- Make a copy of the Metric Conversions activity sheet for each student.

Activity 2: Conversion Factors
- Make a copy of the Conversion Factors activity sheet for each student.

Presenting the Math Concepts

1. Introduce the new terms:

   conversion factor A fraction equal to 1, whose numerator and denominator represent the same quantity but use different units.

   foot (ft) An English unit of measuring distance equal to 12 inches and 0.3 meter.

   gram (g) Basic metric unit for measuring mass.

   length The measurement from one point to another.

   liter (L) Basic metric unit for measuring volume.

   mass The amount of material in a substance.

   measure The process of finding the amount of something.

   meter (m) Basic metric unit for measuring length.

   metric conversion The change from one metric unit to another.

   unit An amount used as a standard of measurement.

   volume The amount of space taken up by an object or enclosed by the object; the amount a container can hold.

2. Explore the new terms:
   - The metric system is a decimal system of measuring.
   - Meter, m (length), liter, L (volume), and gram, g (mass) are the basic units (amounts used as a standard of measurement) in the metric system.
   - The four commonly used metric prefixes are kilo, centi, deci, and milli. Students need to be familiar with these prefixes and their relation to the basic unit.
   - Metric conversion is the change from one metric unit to another. Changing the unit does not change the value of the measurement. For example, 1 meter is the same distance as 100 centimeters.
   - When you multiply a quantity by a conversion factor, only its unit changes, not its value.
   - When converting a unit, choose a conversion factor whose denominator is the same as the unit being changed. For example, to convert 5 minutes to seconds, the conversion factor would be 60 seconds/1 minute. The calculations would be 5 minutes × 60 seconds/1 minute = 300 seconds. When you multiply and divide by the same unit, such as minutes in this problem, the unit cancels out, leaving only the unit of seconds.
   - Another way to make metric conversions is to use the Metric Prefix Line, as shown in Activity 1: Metric Conversions.

EXTENSION

Students can use multiple conversion factors. For example:

Use three conversion factors to determine the number of minutes in 2 years.

2 yr × 365 days/1 yr = 730 days

730 days × 24 hr/1 day = 17,520 hr

17,520 hr × 60 min /1 hr = ?

Answer: 1,051,200 min

Sample Problems

1. Use your age at your last birthday and four conversion factors to determine the number of seconds since your birth.

   age × 365 days/1 yr × 24 hr/day × 60 min/1 hr × 60 sec/1 min = ?

2. Use four conversion factors to change 3 feet to millimeters.

   3 ft × 12 in/1 ft × 2.5 cm/1 in × 1 m/100 cm × 1,000 mm/1 m = ?

   3 × 12 × 2.5 × 1,000/100 = 900 mm

ANSWERS

Activity 1: Metric Conversions

1. 235 mm
2. 23.5 kg
3. 2.599 L
4. 0.0000076 km
5. 0.145 km
6. 560 mL
7. 3.45987 hg
8. 0.0372 kg
9. 0.04 dl
10. 0.987 dag

Activity 2: Conversion Factors

1. 1 yd/3 ft, 3 ft/1 yd
2. 1 in/2.5 cm, 2.5 cm/1 in
3. 1 min/60 sec, 60 sec/1 min
4. 1 hr/60 min, 60 min/1 hr
5. 1 yr/365 days, 365 days/1 yr
6. 300 cm
7. 192 hr
8. 2 hr
9. 2 m
10. 10 in

ACTIVITY 1

Metric Conversions

Measure is the process of finding the amount of something, such as **length** (the measurement from one point to another), **mass** (the amount of material in a substance), and **volume** (the amount of space taken up by an object or enclosed by an object). The **metric system** is a decimal system of measurements. **Meter (m)** (length), **liter (L)** (volume), and **gram (g)** (mass) are the basic **units** (amounts used as a standard of measurement) in the metric system. **Metric conversion** is the change from one metric unit to another. Changing the unit does not change the value of the measurement. One way to do metric conversions is to use the Metric Prefix Line.

Practice Problems

Use the Metric Prefix Line to make the following metric conversions:

1. 8 dm = _____ mm

2. 45,000 cg = _____ hg

    1. Think!

Metric Prefix Line

kilo (k)	hecto (h)	deka (da)	basic unit	deci (d)	centi (c)	milli (m)

- What is the starting prefix? (deci, d)
- What is the final prefix, which is the prefix for the answer? (milli, m)
- On the Metric Prefix Line, count the number of places and note the direction from the starting prefix to the final prefix. How many places are there from deci to milli, and in which direction? (Two places to the right.)
- Move the decimal point of the starting number the same number of places determined in the previous step and in the same direction. What is the new number if the decimal for 8 dm (8 decimeters) is moved to the right two places?

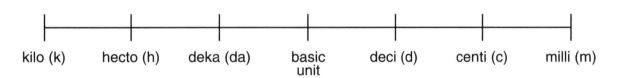

$$8\,00 = 800$$

Answer: 8 dm = 800 mm

2. Think!

- How many places from centi to hecto, and in which direction? (Four places to the left.)
- What is the new number if the decimal for 45,000 cg is moved to the left four places?

Answer: 45,000 cg = 4.5 hg

On Your Own

Use the Metric Prefix Line to make the following metric conversions.

1. 23.5 cm = _____ mm

2. 23,500 g = _____ kg

3. 2,599 mL = _____ L

4. 0.76 cm = _____ km

5. 1.45 hm = _____ km

6. 0.56 L = _____ mL

7. 345,987 mg = _____ hg

8. 0.372 hg = _____ kg

9. 0.4 cl = _____ dl

10. 98.7 dg = _____ dag

Name _____

ACTIVITY 2

Conversion Factors

A **conversion factor** is a fraction equal to 1, whose numerator and denominator represent the same quantity but use different units. For example, a **foot** is an English unit of measuring distance equal to 12 inches and 0.3 meter. So multiplying a quantity by a conversion factor changes only its units, not its value.

Practice Problems

Use a conversion factor to convert each quantity to the given units.

1. 3 feet to inches

Think!

- 1 ft = 12 in

- A conversion factor is a fraction equal to 1 in which the numerator equals the denominator (1 foot is the same amount as 12 inches). Two conversion factors involving the pair of units feet and inches are 1 ft/12 in and 12 in/1 ft.

- When converting a unit, choose a conversion factor whose denominator is the same as the unit being changed. The conversion factor to change feet to inches is 12 in/1 ft.

- Start with the unit to be changed, then multiply by the conversion factor:

  3 ft × 12 in/1 ft = ?

- When you divide and multiply by the same unit, the unit cancels out. So the problem becomes:

  3 × 12 in = ?

Answer: 36 in

2. 24 inches to feet

Think!

- To change inches to feet, use the conversion factor with inches in the denominator, 1 ft/12 in.

- Start with the quantity in the problem, then multiply by the conversion factor:

  24 in × 1 ft/12 in = ?
  24 × $\frac{1}{12}$ ft = ?

Answer: 2 ft

3. 2 feet to meters

Think!

- Use the conversion factor, 0.3 m/1 ft.

- 2 ft × 0.3 m/1 ft = ?
  2 × 0.3 m = ?

Answer: 0.6 m

© 2005 by John Wiley & Sons, Inc.

On Your Own

Using the Unit Comparison Data table, write two conversion factors for each pair of units.

1. yard, feet _____

2. inches, centimeters _____

3. minutes, seconds _____

4. hours, minutes _____

5. years, days _____

UNIT COMPARISON DATA	
1 foot, ft	12 inch, in
1 yard, yd	3 feet, ft
1 inch	2.54 centimeters, cm
1 minute, min	60 seconds, sec
1 hour, hr	60 minutes, min
1 day	24 hours, hr
1 week, wk	7 days
1 year, yr	365 days

Use conversion factors to convert each quantity to the given units.

6. 3 meters to centimeters _____

7. 8 days to hours _____

8. 120 minutes to hours _____

9. 2,000 millimeters to meters _____

10. 25 centimeters to inches _____

Weight and Mass

TEACHING TIPS

Benchmarks

By the end of grade 5, students should be able to
- Estimate and measure weight using units of ounces, pounds, and tons.
- Estimate mass using units of milligrams, grams, and kilograms.

By the end of grade 8, students should be able to
- Convert measures within the same measurement system.

In this chapter, students are expected to
- Estimate weight and mass measurements.
- Determine how the weight of a specific mass would vary on different planets due to changes in gravity.

Preparing the Materials

Activity 1: Weight
- Make a copy of the Weight activity sheet for each student.

Activity 2: Mass
- Make a copy of the Mass activity sheet for each student.

Investigation: How Much?
- Make a copy of the How Much? investigation sheet for each student.
- Bring in a bathroom scale.

Presenting the Math Concepts

1. Introduce the new terms:

   force A push or a pull.

   gravity The force of attraction between objects in the universe; the force that pulls things on or near Earth's surface toward the center of Earth.

   newton (n) A metric unit of weight; 4.5 newtons equal 1 pound.

   ounce (oz) An English unit of weight equal to $\frac{1}{16}$ pound.

   pound (lb) An English unit of weight equal to 16 ounces.

   ton (T) An English unit of weight equal to 2,000 pounds.

   weight The measure of gravity pulling on an object.

2. Explore the new terms:
   - An apple falls from a tree and hits the ground because Earth's gravity is pulling the apple toward the center of Earth.
   - When you stand on a bathroom scale, the scale measures the amount of gravity pulling you toward the center of Earth. In other words, the scale measures your weight.
   - Mass is often compared to weight, but while weight changes depending on the amount of gravity on an object, mass does not change.
   - Weight depends on mass, which is how much matter is being measured. As the amount of matter (mass) increases, weight increases.
   - Use the formula $n = p \times 4.5$ to convert pounds (p) to newtons (n).
   - On Earth, because of the amount of pull of Earth's gravity, 1 kg (1,000 g) of mass weighs 2.2 lb. An astronaut with a body mass of 105 kg would weigh 198 lb on Earth. On the Moon this same person's mass would not change, but his weight would be only 33 lb. This is because the Moon's gravity is about $\frac{1}{6}$ that of Earth.
   - A bathroom scale is used to determine the weight of a person. Any change in the person's weight indicates a gain or loss in matter, thus a gain or loss of mass. For example, if a person's weight changes from 66 lb (30 kg) to 77 lb (35 kg), there is a gain of 5 kg of matter, thus a gain of 11 lb (5 kg $\times$ 2.2 lb/kg = 11 lb).

EXTENSIONS

Use scientific notations to compare masses.

1. Positive scientific notations:

   Which has a greater mass: box A, with a mass of 4×10^7 g, or box B, with a mass of 5×10^4 g?

A. **Think!**
   - Write out the number for each mass.
   - Since the scientific notations are positive, move the decimal place of each number to the right a total number of spaces equal to the magnitude of the power of 10 for the number.

   mass of box A = 4×10^7 g = 40,000,000 g

   mass of box B = 5×10^4 g = 50,000 g

   Answer: Box A has more mass than box B.

B. **Think!**

- Since both exponents are positive, another way to compare the masses is to compare the size of the exponents. The larger the positive exponent is, the larger the number. 4×10^7 has a larger exponent than 5×10^4.

Answer: Box A has more mass than box B.

2. Negative scientific notations:

Which has less weight: a paper clip weighing 2.2×10^{-3} lb, or a piece of paper weighing 4×10^{-5} lb?

A. **Think!**

- Write out the number for each weight.

- Since the scientific notations are negative, move the decimal place of each number to the left a total number of spaces equal to the magnitude of the power of 10 for the number.

weight of the paper clip = 2.2×10^{-3} lb = 0.0022 lb

weight of the paper = 4×10^{-5} lb = 0.00004 lb

Answer: The piece of paper has less weight than the paper clip.

B. **Think!**

- Since both exponents are negative, another way to compare the weights is to compare the size of the exponents. The larger the negative exponent, the smaller the number. 4×10^{-5} has a larger negative exponent than 2.2×10^{-3}.

Answer: The piece of paper has less weight than the paper clip.

ANSWERS

Activity 1: Weight

1. C

2. A

3. A

4. a. ½ oz

   b. 1½ T

5. a. 1 lb

   b. 9 n

Activity 2: Mass

1. salt

2. Tom

3. a. kg

   b. g

   c. g

Weight

A **force** is a push or a pull. **Gravity** is the force of attraction between objects in the universe; it is the force that pulls things on or near Earth's surface toward the center of Earth. On Earth, **weight** is the measure of Earth's gravity pulling on an object. Weight depends on the mass of an object, which is the amount of matter making up the object. As the amount of matter increases, weight increases. Common weight units in the English system are **tons (T)**, **pounds (lb)**, and **ounces (oz)**. In the metric measuring system, **newton (n)** is a common weight unit.

Practice Problems

1. Which unit of weight—ounce, pound, or ton—is a reasonable unit for each of the figures A, B, and C?

WEIGHT EQUIVALENTS	
Weight Unit	**Equivalent Weight Unit**
ton (T)	2,000 lb
pound (lb)	16 oz, 4.5 n

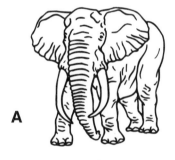

A

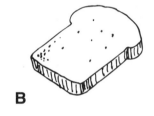

B

C

Think!
- Order the weight units from least to greatest: ounce, pound, ton.
- Order the objects from least to greatest weight: bread slice, bicycle, elephant.

Answers: A, ton; B, ounce; C, pound.

2. Choose the better estimate for the weight of a hippopotamus: 3 lb or 3 T.

Think!
- A loaf of bread weighs about 1 lb. Three loaves of bread would weigh about 3 lb.
- A hippopotamus weighs much more than three loaves of bread, so it cannot weigh 3 lb.

Answer: 3 tons

3. Choose the better estimate for the weight of a baby: 10 lb or 10 oz.

Think!
- A slice of bread weighs about 1 oz. A loaf of bread weighs about 1 lb.
- A baby weighs more than 10 bread slices, but could weigh as much as 10 loaves of bread.

Answer: 10 lb

12 **ACTIVITY 1 (continued)**

On Your Own

1. Circle the figure that most likely weighs 2 lb.

A   B    C

2. Circle the box that weighs more, A or B.

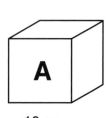 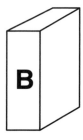

10 oz   ½ lb

3. Circle the animal that weighs less, A or B.

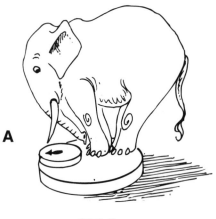 

900 lbs   1½ T

4. Circle the better estimate of weight for each object.

    a. Bird feather   **b.** Car

       ½ oz or ½ lb   1½ lb or 1½ T

5. Circle the heavier weight.

    a. 1 n or 1 lb   **b.** 9 n or 16 oz

Name _____

ACTIVITY 2

Mass

Mass is the amount of matter making up an object. Mass is generally measured in metric units. Gram (g) is the basic metric unit for measuring mass.

1. Which of the bags, A, B, or C, would most likely balance the child on the seesaw?

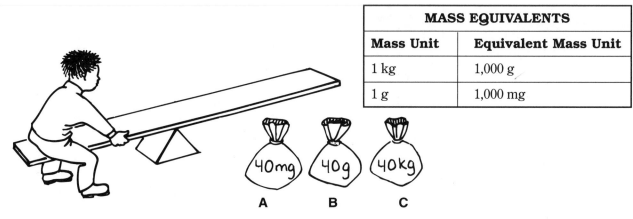

MASS EQUIVALENTS	
Mass Unit	**Equivalent Mass Unit**
1 kg	1,000 g
1 g	1,000 mg

Think!

- Put the masses in order from largest to smallest: 40 kg, 40 g, 40 mg.
- 40 mg is the mass of about 4 fleas, and 40 g is the mass of about 40 paper clips.
- A kg is a little more than 2 lb, so 40 kg is a little more than 80 lb.
- A child's mass is more than 40 fleas or 40 paper clips, but could be around 80 lb, so the bag with a mass of 40 kg would best balance the child.

Answer: Bag C would balance the child.

2. If a penny has a mass of 3 g and the mass of a dog is 3 kg, which mass unit, gram (g) or kilogram (kg), is a reasonable unit to use for the mass of each object listed?

    a. grape   **b.** orange   **c.** cat   **d.** tennis ball

Think!

- The grape, orange, and tennis ball would be closer to the mass of the penny than the mass of the dog, so they would be measured in grams.
- The cat would be closer to the mass of the dog than the mass of the penny, so it would be measured in kilograms.

Answers: a. gram, b. gram, c. kilogram, d. gram

On Your Own

1. Circle the figure that has the greater mass.

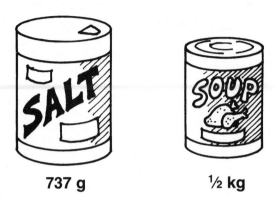

737 g   ½ kg

2. Circle the name of the one who is lifting more mass, Tom or Deano.

Tom   Deano

3. If a grape has a mass of about 1 g and a quart (liter) of water has a mass of about 1 kg, which mass unit, gram (g) or kilogram (kg), is a reasonable unit for each object?

a. table _____   **b.** dime _____   **c.** cookie _____

How Much?

PURPOSE

To determine your weight in pounds and newtons on different planets.

Materials

bathroom scale measuring in pounds
calculator
pencil

Procedure

A. Weight in pounds

1. Determine your weight (F_{wt}) on Earth in pounds by weighing yourself on the bathroom scale.

2. Use the formula $W = F_{wt} \times$ G.R. to determine your weight in pounds on each of the planets in our solar system. Do this by multiplying your weight (F_{wt}) on Earth by each planet's gravity rate (G.R.). (See the Weight Data table.) For example, if you weigh 88 lb (40 kg) on Earth, your weight on Mercury would be w = 88 lb × 0.38 = 33.44 lb.

3. Fill in the weights in pounds for the other planets on the Weight Data table.

B. Weight in newtons

1. A newton (n) is a metric unit for weight. Calculate the weight on each planet in newtons using the formula n = p × 4.5, where p means pounds. For example, the weight on Mercury in newtons would be n = 33.44 pounds × 4.5 = 150.48 n.

2. Fill in the weights in newtons on the Weight Data table.

Results

Your weight varies from one planet to the next.

Why?

Your weight on each planet is a measure of the planet's gravity, which is the force (push or pull) that pulls things on or near a planet toward its center. The gravity rate (G.R.) of the planets is their gravity compared to Earth's, thus Earth's G.R. is equal to 1, commonly called 1 g. The more massive the planet, the greater is its gravity. Jupiter, with the greatest G.R., is the most massive of the planets. Pluto, with the least G.R., is the least massive.

WEIGHT DATA			
		Weight on Planet (w)	
Planet	**Gravity Rate (G.R.)**	**Pounds (lb)**	**Newtons (n)**
Mercury	0.38	33.44	150.48
Venus	0.90		
Earth	1.00	88	396
Mars	0.38		
Jupiter	2.54		
Saturn	1.16		
Uranus	0.92		
Neptune	1.19		
Pluto	0.06		

Temperature

TEACHING TIPS

Benchmarks

By the end of grade 5, students should be able to
- Measure to solve problems involving temperature.
- Explain and record observations using pictures and objects.

By the end of grade 8, students should be able to
- Select and use appropriate tools or formulas to measure and to solve problems involving temperature.
- Identify and apply mathematics to everyday experiences.

In this chapter, students are expected to
- Read a Celsius and a Fahrenheit thermometer.
- Make and use models of a Fahrenheit and a Celsius thermometer.

Preparing the Materials

Activity: Temperature
- Make a copy of the Temperature activity sheet for each student.

Investigation: Up and Down
- Make a copy of the Up and Down investigation sheet for each student.
- Make a copy of the Thermometer Patterns for each student.

Presenting the Math Concepts

1. Introduce the new terms:

    Celsius degree (°C) A metric unit of measuring temperature.

    Celsius scale A metric temperature scale in which the freezing point of water is 0° and the boiling point is 100°.

    degree (°) The unit of measuring temperature.

    Fahrenheit degree (°F) An English unit of measuring temperature.

    Fahrenheit scale An English temperature scale in which the freezing point of water is 32° and the boiling point is 212°.

    temperature A measurement of how cold or hot an object is.

    thermometer An instrument that numerically measures temperature.

2. Explore the new terms:
    - In 1593, Galileo Galilei (1564–1642) designed the first crude thermometer, which he called a "thermoscope." The thermoscope did not have a scale, so only qualitative measurement, such as hot, warm, cool, or cold, could be made. The thermoscope and modern thermometers with liquids are based on the fact that fluids (gases and liquids) expand when heated and contract when cooled.
    - Daniel Gabriel Fahrenheit (1686–1736), a German scientist, introduced the alcohol thermometer in 1709 and the mercury thermometer in 1714. He introduced a temperature scale, now called the Fahrenheit scale, in 1724.
    - The degree unit measures temperature. For example, 10°F is read as "10 degrees Fahrenheit."
    - The Swedish astronomer Anders Celsius (1701–1744) devised the Celsius thermometer scale, which originally had 0° as the boiling point of water and 100° as water's freezing point. This scale was soon reversed so that 0° was water's freezing point and 100° was water's boiling point, which is the scale that is used today.
    - At one time, mercury was the primary liquid in modern thermometers. Since thermometers do get broken and mercury is toxic (poisonous), people started using other liquids in thermometers, such as alcohol and dyes. More recently, since alcohol is flammable, people have been using a safer mixture of a vegetable oil-type liquid and dyes.
    - Fahrenheit scales generally have five divisions between each printed number. Each division equals 2°.
    - Celsius scales generally have ten divisions between each printed number. Each division equals 1°.
    - Body temperature is about 98.6°F and about 37°C.
    - Room temperature is about 75°F and about 24°C.

EXTENSIONS

1. Encourage the class to work independently with the thermometer models. Observe the progress of students individually to make sure they can find the

numbers on the models and understand the value of each division on the scales. Write more temperatures on the chalkboard that can be demonstrated by the models. The models can be used to evaluate student understanding. Do this by giving each student temperatures to find on the two models. Watch as the student moves the strip to place it on or between the marks for the given temperatures.

2. Students can convert between Celsius and Fahrenheit units using these formulas.

Celsius to Fahrenheit:

°F = (1.8 × °C) + 32

Example: Change 100°C to °F.

°F = (1.8 × 100) + 32
= 180 + 32
= 212°F

Fahrenheit to Celsius:

°C = (°F − 32) ÷ 1.8

Example: Change 212°F to °C.

°C = (212 − 32) ÷ 1.8
= 180 ÷ 1.8
= 100°C

ANSWERS

Activity: Temperature

I.

1. **A.** 8°F
   B. 34°C
   C. 105°F
   D. 104.5°C

2. **A.** below freezing
   B. above freezing
   C. above freezing
   D. above freezing

3. **A.** below boiling
   B. below boiling
   C. below boiling
   D. above boiling

4. **A.** 3°F
   B. 29°C
   C. 100°F
   D. 99.5°C

II.

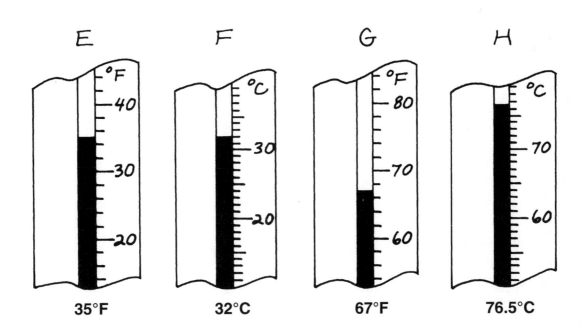

13 ACTIVITY

Temperature

Temperature is a measurement of how cold or hot an object is. A **thermometer** is an instrument that numerically measures temperature in units called **degrees (°)**. The number 32° is read as "32 degrees." A **Fahrenheit scale** is an English temperature scale in which the freezing point of water is 32° and the boiling point is 212°. A **Fahrenheit degree (°F)** is an English unit of measuring temperature. A **Celsius scale** is a metric temperature scale in which the freezing point of water is 0° and the boiling point is 100°. A **Celsius degree (°C)** is a metric unit of measuring temperature.

Practice Problems

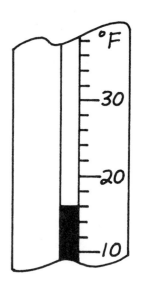

1. Read the thermometer and record the temperature.

Think!

- °F on the thermometer indicates that the temperature is being measured in the English unit of Fahrenheit and is read as "degrees Fahrenheit."
- The numbers 10, 20, and 30 marked on the scale are read as "10°F (10 degrees Fahrenheit)," "20°F (20 degrees Fahrenheit)," and "30°F (30 degrees Fahrenheit)."
- There are 10° between each numbered mark and five divisions between each numbered mark; thus each unnumbered division is equal to 2°F.
- The height of the liquid in the thermometer is at the third division above 10°F. Thus the reading on the thermometer is 10°F + 6°F.

Answer: The thermometer reads 16°F.

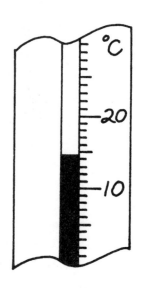

2. Read the thermometer and record the temperature.

Think!

- °C on the thermometer indicates that the temperature is being measured in the metric unit of Celsius.
- The numbers 10 and 20 marked on the scale are read as "10°C (10 degrees Celsius)" and "20°C (20 degrees Celsius)."
- There are 10° between each numbered mark and ten divisions between each numbered mark; thus each division is equal to 1°F.
- The height of the liquid in the thermometer is halfway between 14°C and 15°C and can be read as "14½°C" or "14.5°C."

Answer: The thermometer reads 14.5°C.

On Your Own

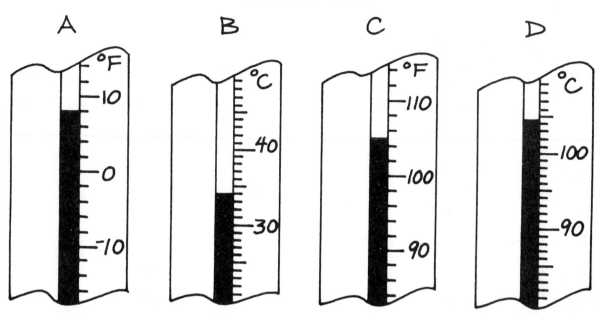

I. Answer the following for thermometers A, B, C, and D.

   1. Read each thermometer and write the temperature indicated in °C or °F.

   2. Is the temperature above or below the freezing point of water?

   3. Is the temperature above or below the boiling point of water?

   4. What would be the reading if the temperature dropped 5 degrees?

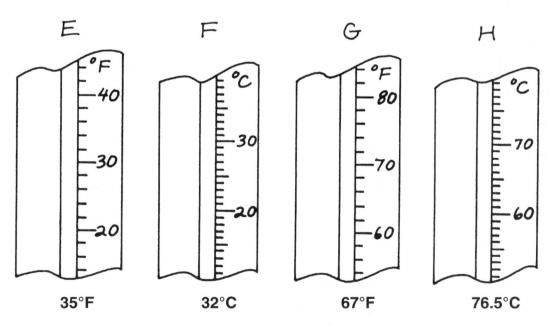

II. For thermometers E, F, G, and H, color in the thermometers so that each shows the indicated temperatures.

Up and Down

PURPOSE

To make a model of a Celsius and a Fahrenheit thermometer.

Materials

red crayon
Celsius thermometer and Fahrenheit
 thermometer patterns
scissors
ruler
pen
transparent tape
pencil

Procedure

1. To make a model of a Celsius thermometer use the following steps:

- Color the liquid strip and bulb portion of the Celsius thermometer pattern red.

- Cut out the two indicated areas.

- Cut along the dotted line to separate the liquid strip from the other section.

- Lay the ruler along each of the fold lines, then trace the lines with the pen. This is called scoring, which makes it easier to fold along the line.

- Fold the paper along fold line 1, then along fold line 2, and secure the folded sections together with tape.

- Insert the liquid strip in the liquid strip slot so that the colored side of the strip is visible through the openings in the front of the model.

- Use the pencil to number the scale of the thermometer, starting with 0°.

- Move the colored strip so that the top of the strip is between the ninth and tenth divisions on the scale. Determine the temperature reading with the strip in this position.

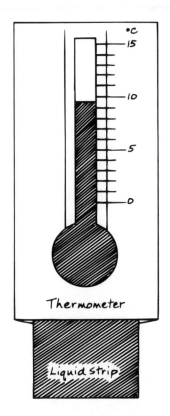

Thermometer

Liquid strip

2. Using the Fahrenheit thermometer pattern, repeat step 1.

Results

The temperature reading on the Celsius thermometer is 9.5°C, and the reading on the Fahrenheit thermometer is 19°F.

Thermometer Pattern, Celsius

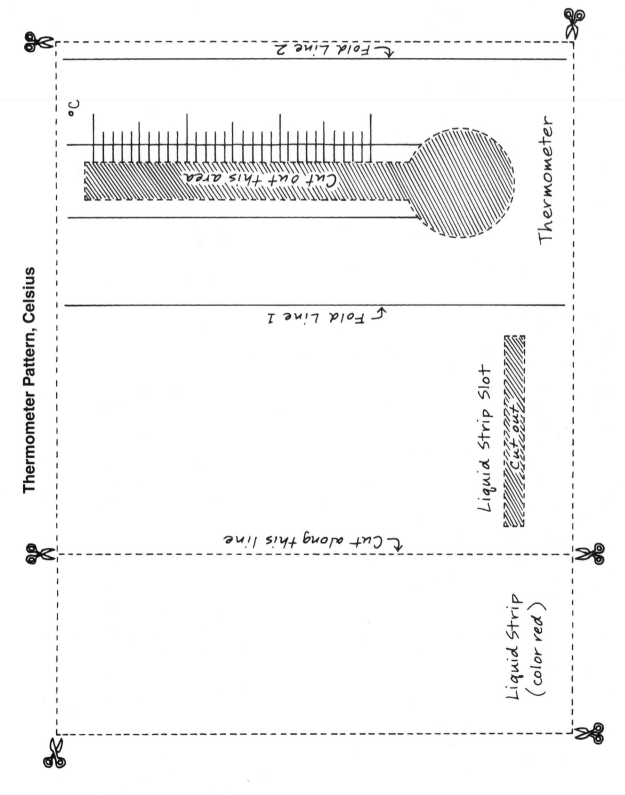

°C

Fold Line 2

Cut out this area

Thermometer

Fold Line 1

Liquid Strip Slot

Cut out

Cut along this line

Liquid Strip
(color red)

Thermometer Pattern, Fahrenheit

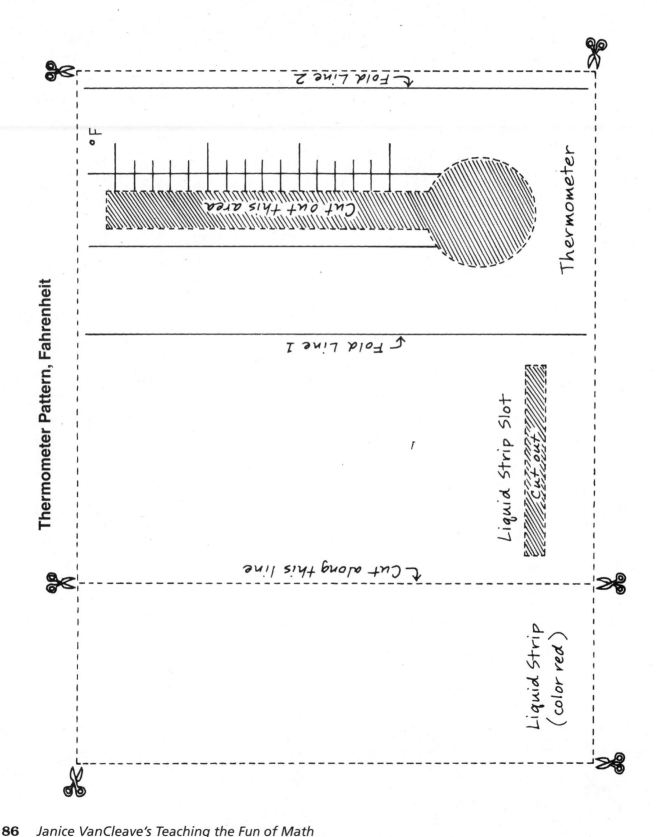

°F

Fold Line 2

Cut out this area

Thermometer

Fold Line 1

Liquid Strip Slot

Cut out

Cut along this line

Liquid Strip
(color red)

Geometry

Geometry is the study of shapes and figures. It uses numbers and symbols to describe the properties of these shapes and the relationships between them. This section explores two different kinds of shapes: **plane figures** (geometric figures that lie on a flat surface) and **solid figures** (geometric figures that have three dimensions and volume). Understanding geometry is important because questions such as What is its shape?, How big is it?, and Will it fit? are all part of everyday life. Geometry provides the skills needed to find the answers to such questions.

Lines

TEACHING TIPS

Benchmarks

By the end of grade 5, students should be able to
• Identify lines.

By the end of grade 8, students should be able to
• Identify critical attributes of lines.

In this chapter, students are expected to
• Show and name lines.

Preparing the Materials

Activity: Lines
• Make a copy of the Lines activity sheet for each student.

Investigation: Optical Illusion
• Make a copy of the Optical Illusion investigation sheet for each student.

Presenting the Math Concepts

1. Introduce the new terms:

   line A straight path that can go on forever in both directions.

   parallel Being equidistant apart at all points.

2. Explore the new terms:
   • A common use of the word line is a mark made by a pen, pencil, or other tool on a surface. This line can be of any shape or length. It can be straight or curved, such as the tracing around your hand.
   • The geometric definition of line is a straight path with no endpoints. This continuation is indicated by an arrow at each end of a straight line. It is the geometric definition that will be used in this chapter.
   • A geometric line can be identified by naming any two points on the line, such as points T and A in the diagram. The name of the line is read "line TA" or "line AT." The symbol for a line includes the names of any two points on the line with a line with an arrow at each end drawn above it. The symbol for the line in the figure is $\overleftrightarrow{TA}$ or $\overleftrightarrow{AT}$.

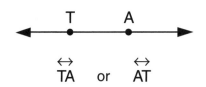

$\overleftrightarrow{TA}$ or $\overleftrightarrow{AT}$

• Parallel lines never cross because they extend in the same direction and are equidistant at all points, as in the following example.

EXTENSION

A *plane* is a flat surface that can extend in all directions without end. Lines that do not lie in the same plane are called *skew lines*. Students can identify skew lines in magazine pictures, such as lines that form 3-D structures like buildings.

ANSWERS

Activity: Lines

1. **a.** The top diagram should be circled.
   b. line BX or line XB
   c. $\overleftrightarrow{BX}$ or $\overleftrightarrow{XB}$

2. **a.** The diagram on the right should be circled.
   b. line RS or line SR
   c. $\overleftrightarrow{RS}$ or $\overleftrightarrow{SR}$

3. **a.**

   b.

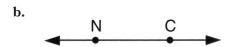

© 2005 by John Wiley & Sons, Inc.

ACTIVITY

Lines

A **line** is a straight path that can go on forever in both directions. In a diagram, a line is shown by arrows at the two ends of the line. A line can be identified by naming any two points on the line. The symbol for a line includes the names of any two points on the line, with a line with an arrow at each end drawn above it. **Parallel** lines are equidistant apart at all points.

Practice Problems

1. Study diagrams A and B and answer the following:

   a. Which diagram, A or B, represents a line?

   b. Name the line.

   c. Give the symbol for the line.

a. Think!

• Which example shows a straight path with arrows at each end?

Answer: Diagram B represents a line.

b. Think!

• What are the names of two points on the line?

Answer: The name of the line is line WV or line VW.

c. Think!

• The symbol for a line gives the names of any two points on the line, with a line with an arrow at each end drawn above it.

Answer: The symbol for the line is $\overleftrightarrow{WV}$ or $\overleftrightarrow{VW}$.

2. Which diagram, C or D, represents parallel lines?:

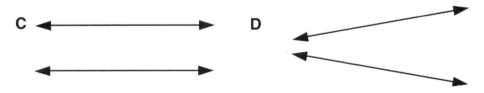

Think!

• Parallel lines are equidistant at all points.

Answer: Diagram C represents parallel lines.

On Your Own

Study the diagrams for problems 1 and 2 and answer the following for each:

a. Circle the diagram that represents a line.

b. Write the name of the line on the blank provided.

c. Give the symbol for the line on the blank provided.

1.

B   X

C   Z

W   N

Name _____

Symbol _____

2.

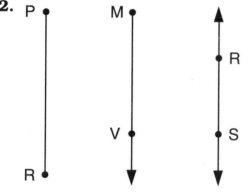

Name _____

Symbol _____

3. Draw a line for each symbol. Make the lines parallel to each other.

a. $\overleftrightarrow{JV}$

b. $\overleftrightarrow{NC}$

14 **INVESTIGATION**

Optical Illusion

PURPOSE

To use lines to demonstrate an optical illusion.

Materials

ruler
2 pencils
copy paper

Procedure

1. Use the ruler and one of the pencils to draw a 2-inch (5-cm) horizontal line in the center and near the top edge of the paper.

2. Draw a second line of equal length, parallel with and 1 inch (2.5 cm) below the first line. Label the top line A and the lower line B.

3. Lay the two pencils so they are parallel with each other, with their eraser ends touching the ends of line A. Note how long lines A and B appear. Do they appear to be the same length?

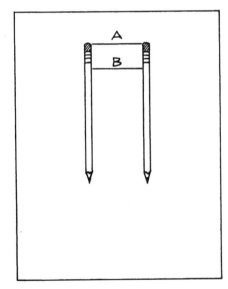

4. With the eraser ends of the pencils still touching the ends of line A, separate the opposite ends of the pencils about 6 inches (15 cm). Again compare the lines and note if one appears to be longer than the other.

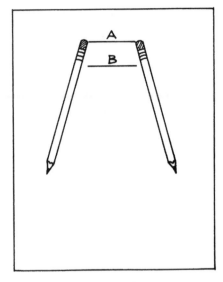

Results

The two lines appear to be the same length when the pencils placed alongside of them are parallel. But line A appears longer when the pencils are not parallel, with the ends of the pencils closer at line A and farther apart at line B.

Why?

Sometimes what we see is not what actually exists. What we see involves more than looking at something with our eyes. The eyes send messages to the brain about the object viewed, and the brain interprets the messages. An incorrect interpretation may cause you to "see" a misleading image, which is called an *optical illusion.* The way the brain interprets the size of the lines you drew is influenced by things that surround the lines, such as the pencils. When the pointed ends of the pencils are separated, line A touches the pencils, and line B appears too short to touch them. Thus line B is interpreted as being shorter. It doesn't matter if you know that the two lines are the same length, your brain takes in all the information and an incorrect interpretation is still made; thus you see an optical illusion.

Line Segments
TEACHING TIPS

Benchmarks

By the end of grade 5, students should be able to
• Identify line segments.

By the end of grade 8, students should be able to
• Identify critical attributes of line segments.

In this chapter, students are expected to
• Show and name line segments.
• Create dot-to-dot art using line segments.

Preparing the Materials

Activity: Line Segments
• Make a copy of the Line Segments activity sheet for each student.

Investigation: Dot-to-Dot
• Make a copy of the Dot-to-Dot investigation sheet for each student.
• Make a copy of the Dot-to-Dot Line Segments sheet for each student.
• Cut one 8-by-8-inch (20-by-20-cm) piece of colored poster board for each student.

Presenting the Math Concepts

1. Introduce the new term:

    line segment A part of a line with two endpoints.

2. Explore the new term:

    • A line segment is named by its endpoints. The name of the line segment below is read "line segment HI" or "line segment IH."

• The symbol for a line segment is the name of the two endpoints, with a line drawn above the name. The symbol for the line segment shown is $\overline{HI}$ or $\overline{IH}$.

EXTENSION

Students can create dot-to-dot art using line segments. They should include a list of the line segments that must be connected to complete the art. Copies of the dot-to-dot art can be made so that students can share their creative ideas.

ANSWERS

Activity: Line Segments

1. **a.** Diagram B should be circled.
   b. line segment CD or DC
   c. $\overline{CD}$ or $\overline{DC}$

2. **a.** Diagram C should be circled.
   b. line segment JV or VJ.
   c. $\overline{JV}$ or $\overline{VJ}$

3. **a.**

b.

15 ACTIVITY

Line Segments

A **line segment** is part of a line with two endpoints. The name of a line segment is the name of the two endpoints. The symbol for a line segment is the name of the two endpoints with a line above it.

Practice Problems

Study diagrams A and B and answer the following:

a. Which diagram, A or B, represents a line segment?

b. Name the line segment.

c. Give the symbol for the line segment.

a. Think!

• Which example shows part of a line segment with two endpoints?

Answer: Diagram A represents a line segment.

b. Think!

• What are the names of the endpoints of the line segment? L and N.

Answer: The name of the line segment is line segment LN or line segment NL.

c. Think!

• The symbol for a line segment is the name of the two endpoints, with a line drawn above the name.

Answer: The symbol for the line segment is $\overline{LN}$ or $\overline{NL}$.

ACTIVITY (continued)

On Your Own

Study the diagrams for problems 1 and 2 and answer the following for each:

a. Circle the diagram that represents a line segment.

b. Write the name of the line segment.

c. Give the symbol for the line segment.

1.

Name _____

Symbol _____

2.

Name _____

Symbol _____

3. Draw a line segment for each symbol.

   a. $\overline{KB}$

   b. $\overline{TR}$

Name

INVESTIGATION

Dot-to-Dot

PURPOSE

To create dot-to-dot art using line segments.

Materials

copy of the Dot-to-Dot Line Segments sheet
ruler
pencil
scissors
bottle of school glue
8-by-8-inch (20-by-20-cm) pieces of colored
    poster board
glitter, your choice of color
paper punch
8-inch (20-cm) piece of colored yarn

Procedure

1. On the diagram, use the ruler and pencil to connect the dots by drawing line segments $\overline{AB}$, $\overline{BC}$, $\overline{CD}$, $\overline{DE}$, $\overline{EF}$, $\overline{FG}$, $\overline{GH}$, $\overline{HI}$, $\overline{IJ}$, and $\overline{JA}$.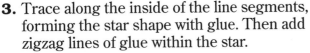

2. Cut out the star design and glue it to the poster board.

3. Trace along the inside of the line segments, forming the star shape with glue. Then add zigzag lines of glue within the star.

4. Cover the glue lines with glitter. Shake off the excess glitter and allow the glue to dry. This may take one or more hours.

5. When the glue is dry, cut along the outside line segments to cut out the design from the poster board.

6. Use the paper punch to make a hole in the top arm of the star.

7. Thread the yarn through the hole and tie the yarn into a loop. The star can be hung from the string.

Result

A design of a star is formed using line segments.

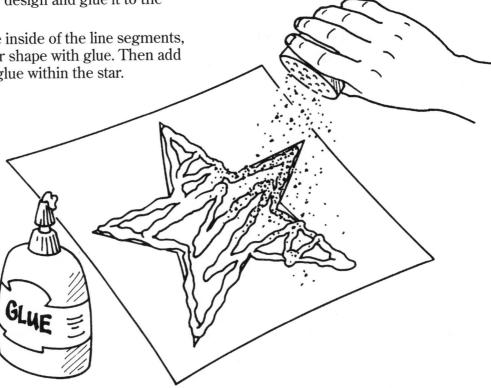

INVESTIGATION (continued)

Dot-to-Dot Line Segments

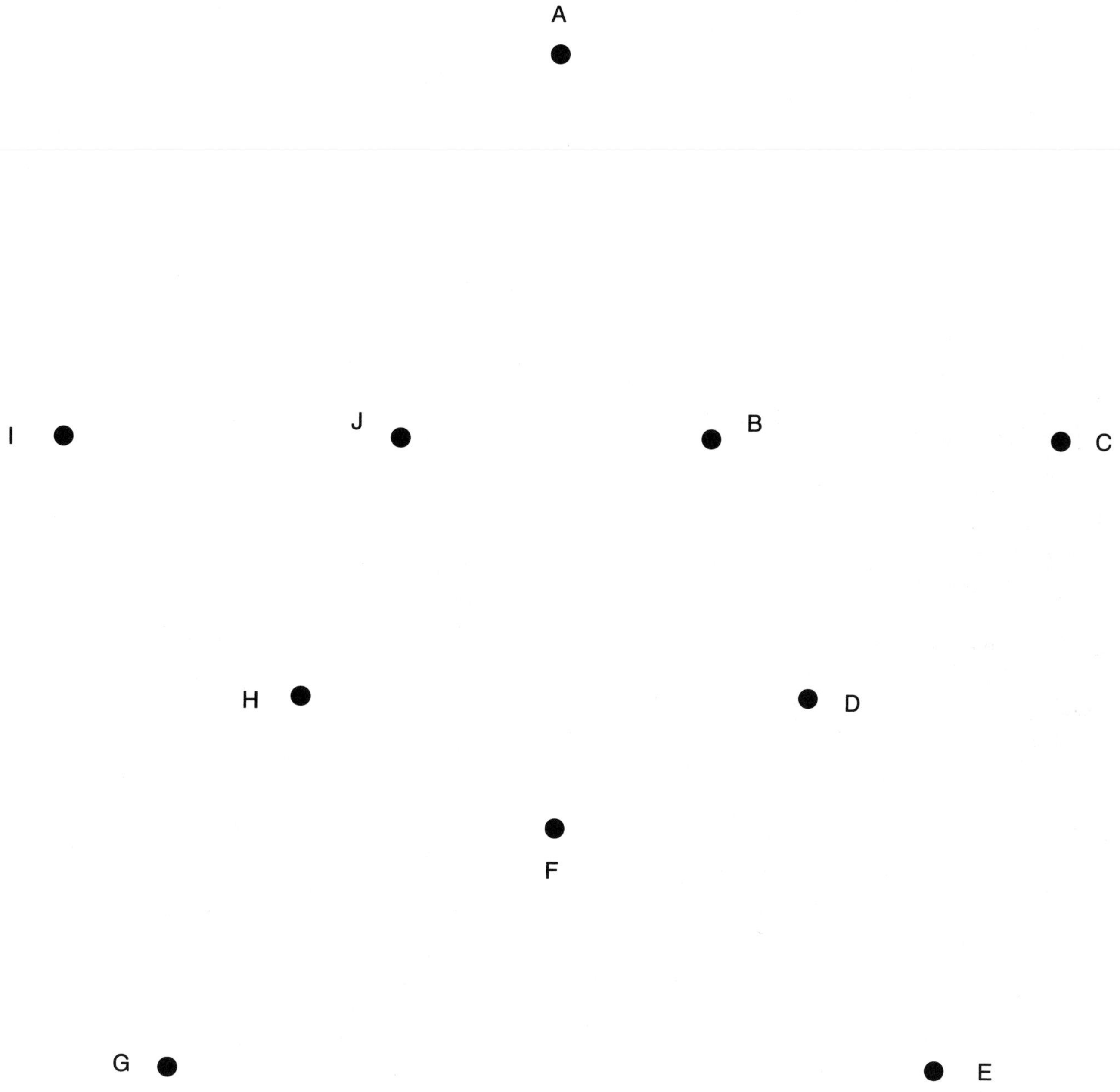

A
●

I ●   J ●   ● B   ● C

H ●   ● D

F
●

G ●   ● E

Rays

TEACHING TIPS

Benchmarks

By the end of grade 5, students should be able to
- Distinguish between lines, line segments, and rays.

By the end of grade 8, students should be able to
- Identify critical attributes of rays.

In this chapter, students are expected to
- Show and name rays.

Preparing the Materials

Activity: Rays
- Make a copy of the Rays activity sheet for each student.

Presenting the Math Concepts

1. Introduce the new term:

   ray A part of a line having only one endpoint.

2. Explore the new term:
   - A ray starts at an endpoint and can go on forever in the direction of a point on the part of the line making up the ray. A ray's name starts with the endpoint and includes the second point. For the ray shown, its name is read "ray HA."

   - A ray's symbol contains the name of the endpoint and one other point on the ray with a line and an arrow at one end. For the ray shown, the symbol is $\overrightarrow{HA}$.
   - Rays can be used to indicate direction. Ray HA starts at H and goes on in the direction of A.

EXTENSION

Rays intersect if they cross or have one end point. The examples show two rays in different directions. Ask students to draw figures with different numbers of rays, such as two, three, four, and five, that intersect at one end point. The distance between the rays as well as the length of the rays will vary, and students may get creative with their diagrams.

ANSWERS

Activity: Rays

1. **a.** Diagram B should be circled.
   b. ray CD
   c. $\overrightarrow{CD}$

2. **a.** Diagram A should be circled.
   b. ray GW
   c. $\overrightarrow{GW}$

3.

Object	Ray diagram	Ray symbol
tree	C N	$\overrightarrow{CN}$
flower	C E	$\overrightarrow{CE}$
squirrel	C S	$\overrightarrow{CS}$
child	C W	$\overrightarrow{CW}$

Rays

A **ray** is a part of a line having only one endpoint. The name of a ray is the name of the end-point and one other point on the line. The symbol for a ray is the letters of the name, with a line with one arrow at the right end above the letters.

Practice Problems

For diagrams A and B:

    a. Which diagram, A or B, represents a ray?

    b. Name the ray.

    c. Give the symbol for the ray.

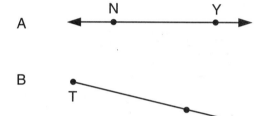

a. Think!

• Which example shows part of a line with an endpoint at one end and an arrow at the other end?

Answer: Diagram B represents a ray.

b. Think!

• What are the names of the endpoint and a second point? T and X.

Answer: The name of the ray is ray TX.

c. Think!

Answer: The symbol for the ray is $\overrightarrow{TX}$.

On Your Own

Study the diagrams for problems 1 and 2 and answer the following for each:

a. Circle the diagram that represents a ray.

b. Name the ray.

c. Give the symbol for the ray.

1.

A A ←——•——————•——→ B

B C •——————————•——→ D

C E •——————————————————• F

2.

A W ←——•——————————————• G

B T •——————————————————• A

C S •——————————————————• D

Name _____

Symbol _____

Name _____

Symbol _____

3. A *compass* is an instrument that indicates direction. Its needle has two ends. One end always points north (N) and the other south (S), as indicated in the diagram. Using the compass directions of north (N), south (S), east (E), and west (W), draw rays showing the direction of each object from the center of the compass (C), and write the symbol for each ray.

Object	Ray Diagram	Ray Symbol
tree		
flower		
squirrel		
child		

Measuring Angles

TEACHING TIPS

Benchmarks

By the end of grade 5, students should be able to
- Identify the mathematics in everyday situations.
- Identify right, acute, and obtuse angles.
- Use tools to measure angles.

By the end of grade 8, students should be able to
- Select and use appropriate tools to solve problems involving angles.

In this chapter, students are expected to
- Use tools to classify and measure angle sizes.
- Estimate angle sizes.

Preparing the Materials

Activity 1: Classifying Angles
- Make a copy of the Classifying Angles activity sheet for each student.
- Transparent rulers with straight edges forming right angles are needed for each student.

Activity 2: Using a Protractor
- Make a copy of the Using a Protractor activity sheet for each student.

Presenting the Math Concepts

1. Introduce the new terms:

   acute angle An angle that measures less than 90 degrees.

   angle Distance formed by two rays that have the same endpoint; also the distance between two intersecting line segments or lines.

   degree (°) The unit of measuring an angle.

   intersect To cross or meet at a single point.

   obtuse angle An angle that measures greater than 90 degrees.

   perpendicular To intersect at a right angle.

   protractor An instrument used to measure the size of an angle.

   right angle An angle that measures 90 degrees.

   straight angle An angle that measures 180 degrees.

   vertex The point where rays, line segments, or lines intersect; also called a corner.

2. Explore the new math terms:
   - Angles are made up of two sides that meet at a common point called the vertex.
   - The symbol ∠ can be used instead of writing the word angle.
   - The unit used in measuring an angle is the degree. One degree is written as 1°.
   - A square is drawn to indicate where rays and line segments meet at a right angle.
   - Intersecting lines and line segments form angles, but parallel lines never form angles because they never meet or cross.

EXTENSIONS

1. A corner of an index card measures 90°. Students can use an index card to find examples of 90° angles in the classroom. A list of objects with 90° angles can be made, such as the corner of a desk or a door frame.

2. Ask students to make drawings of angles such as 30°, 45°, and 90° without looking at labeled diagrams or using a protractor. Once the diagrams have been made, students can determine the accuracy of their estimates by measuring the drawn angles with a protractor.

ANSWERS

Activity 1: Classifying Angles

1. right
2. obtuse
3. acute
4. obtuse
5. straight
6. acute

Activity 2: Using a Protractor

1. **A.** 20°
   B. 140°
   C. 35°
2. 160°

ACTIVITY 1

Classifying Angles

An **angle** is the distance formed by two rays that have the same endpoint; it is also the distance between two intersecting (crossing or meeting at a point) line segments. The point where rays, line segments, or lines intersect is called a corner or a **vertex**. A **degree (°)** is the unit of measuring an angle. Angles are classified by the way their measures compare to 90°. An **acute angle** measures less than 90°. A **right angle** measures 90°. An **obtuse angle** measures greater than 90°. A **straight angle** measures 180°. **Perpendicular** rays, line segments, or lines **intersect** (cross or meet at a single point) one another at right angles.

Practice Problems

Use the corner of a transparent ruler to classify angles A, B, and C as acute, obtuse, or right.

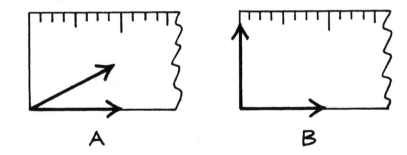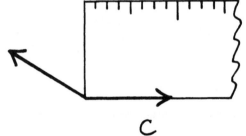

A   B   C

A. Think!
- The corner of the ruler is 90°.
- Lay the ruler on angle A so the bottom edge of the ruler is along one of the angle's rays and the corner of the ruler is touching the vertex of the angle as shown.
- Angle A is smaller than the 90° angle formed by the corner of the ruler.

Answer: Angle A is an acute angle.

B. Think!
- The angle is equal to the 90° angle formed by the corner of the ruler.

Answer: Angle B is a right angle.

C. Think!
- The angle is larger than the 90° angle formed by the corner of the ruler.

Answer: Angle C is an obtuse angle.

On Your Own

Use a transparent ruler with right angle edges to classify each angle below as acute, right, obtuse, or straight.

1. _____

2. _____

3. _____

4. _____

5. _____

6. _____

ACTIVITY 2

Using a Protractor

A **protractor** is an instrument used to measure the size of an angle. The curved edge of a protractor has a scale marked in degrees. Semicircle protractors have a straight edge, with a protractor line connecting the curved scale. There is a hole in the middle of the protractor line.

Practice Problem

Use a protractor to measure ∠ TOM.

Think!

- To measure an angle, place the hole in the middle of the protractor line over the vertex of the angle. Position the protractor so the protractor line is over one side of the angle.

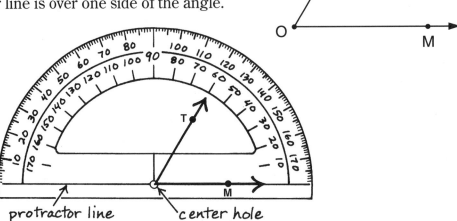

- A ruler or an index card can be used to extend one of the sides when the sides of the angle are too short to cross the scale of the protractor, as in the diagram.

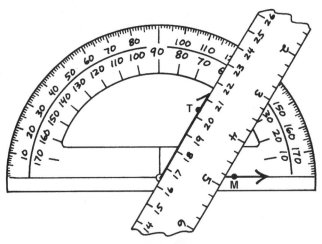

- There are two numbers on the scale where the second ray of the angle crosses. The smaller number is the measure for an acute angle; the larger number is the measure for an obtuse angle.

ACTIVITY 2 (continued)

• The angle being measured is acute, so the angle measurement is the smaller number on the protractor.

Answer: The measure for ∠ TOM is 60°.

On Your Own

1. Use a protractor to measure angles for diagrams A, B, and C.

A. ∠ WRV _____

A

B. ∠ LNR _____

B
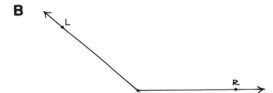

C. ∠ FUN _____

C
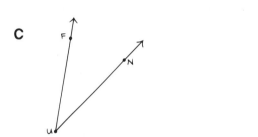

2. Measure the angle of the lounge chair's lifted back.

_____

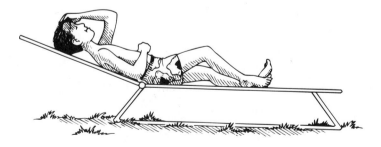

Triangles

TEACHING TIPS

Benchmarks

By the end of grade 5, students should be able to
• Identify characteristics of geometric shapes, including triangles.

By the end of grade 8, students should be able to
• Use properties to classify shapes, including triangles.

In this chapter, students are expected to
• Classify triangles by the measure of their sides.
• Classify triangles by the size of their angles.
• Prove that the sum of the angles of a triangle equals 180°.

Preparing the Materials

Activity: Classifying Triangles
• Make a copy of the Classifying Triangles activity sheet for each student.
• Each student needs a transparent ruler with straight edges.

Investigation: Sum It Up!
• Make a copy of the Sum It Up! investigation sheet for each student.

Presenting the Math Concepts

1. Introduce the new terms:

   acute triangle A triangle in which all the angles are less than 90°.

   congruent Equal in shape or size.

   equilateral triangle A triangle with three congruent sides.

   isosceles triangle A triangle with two congruent sides.

   obtuse triangle A triangle in which one of the angles is greater than 90°.

   plane figure A geometric figure that lies on a flat surface.

   polygon A closed plane figure formed by three or more line segments that do not cross over each other.

   right triangle A triangle with one 90° angle.

   scalene triangle A triangle with no congruent sides.

   triangle A three-sided polygon.

2. Explore the new terms:
   • A closed figure is one that begins and ends at the same point.
   • A triangle is a closed figure made from three line segments.
   • Like angles, triangles can be classified using the terms acute, right, and obtuse.
   • An acute triangle has three acute angles.
   • A right triangle has one right angle. The other two angles are acute.
   • An obtuse triangle has one obtuse angle. The other two angles are acute.
   • The sum of the angles created by the three sides of a triangle is always 180°.

EXTENSIONS

1. Students can use a protractor to measure the angles of triangles in degrees.
2. Students can repeat the Sum It Up! investigation using different types of triangles: right, acute, and obtuse.

ANSWERS

Activity: Classifying Triangles

1. **a.** isosceles
   b. acute
2. **a.** scalene
   b. obtuse
3. **a.** scalene
   b. right
4. **a.** isosceles
   b. obtuse

© 2005 by John Wiley & Sons, Inc.

Classifying Triangles

A **plane figure** is a geometric figure that lies on a flat surface. A **polygon** is a closed plane figure formed by three or more line segments that do not cross over each other. A **triangle** is a three-sided polygon. **Congruent** means equal in shape or size. An **equilateral triangle** has three congruent sides. An **isosceles triangle** has two congruent sides. A **scalene triangle** has no congruent sides. A **right triangle** has one 90° angle. An **acute triangle** has all angles less than 90°. An **obtuse triangle** has one angle greater than 90°.

Practice Problems

1. Classify the triangle by the measure of its sides as equilateral, isosceles, or scalene.

Think!

- Using a ruler to measure the length of the sides of the triangle in the diagram shows that it has two congruent sides.

Answer: The triangle is an isosceles triangle.

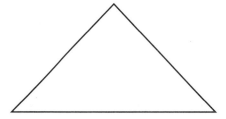

2. Classify the triangle by the measure of its angles as right, acute, or obtuse.

Think!

- Using a protractor, you find that ∠ A in the diagram is equal to 90° and ∠ B and ∠ C are less than 90°.

- What kind of triangle has one 90° angle?

Answer: The triangle is a right triangle.

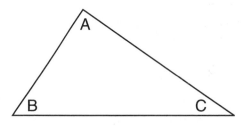

On Your Own

Classify each triangle by:

a. the measure of its sides as equilateral, isosceles, or scalene.

b. the measure of its angles as right, acute, or obtuse.

1. a. _____

    b. _____

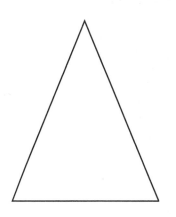

2. a. _____

   b. _____

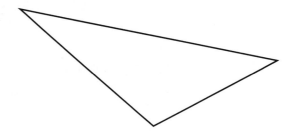

3. a. _____

   b. _____

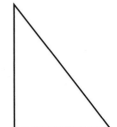

4. a. _____

   b. _____

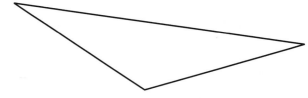

Sum It Up!

PURPOSE

To determine the sum of the angles of a triangle.

Materials

sheet of copy paper
scissors
ruler
pencil

Procedure

1. Fold the paper in half by placing the short sides together. Unfold the paper and cut along the fold line.

2. Use the ruler and pencil to draw a line across the center of one of the paper pieces.

3. Use the ruler and pencil to draw a triangle as large as possible on the second piece.

4. Label the angles of the triangle A, B, and C and shade one corner of each as shown.

5. Cut out the triangle.

6. Cut off about 1 inch (2.5 cm) of the tip of each triangle as shown.

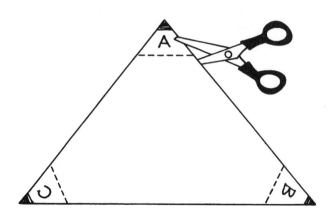

7. On the line drawn on the first piece of copy paper, place all the triangle tips together at one point. Note the angle that the combined pieces form.

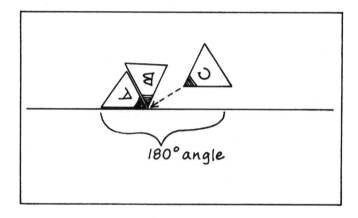

Result

The combined angles from the triangle form a straight angle, which measures 180°, but the sides of the triangles may vary in length.

Why?

Since the sum of the angles of any triangle totals 180°, this investigation will work for any triangle no matter the size of the angles.

Quadrilaterals

TEACHING TIPS

Benchmarks

By the end of grade 5, students should be able to
- Identify important characteristics of quadrilaterals.
- Use charts and diagrams to find patterns, such as relationships between quadrilaterals.

By the end of grade 8, students should be able to
- Identify quadrilaterals by the special characteristics and relationships of their sides and angles.

In this chapter, students are expected to
- Learn to identify different quadrilaterals and their specific characteristics.

Preparing the Materials

Activity 1: Quadrilaterals
- Make a copy of the Quadrilaterals activity sheet for each student.

Activity 2: Parallelograms
- Make a copy of the Parallelograms activity sheet for each student.

Presenting the Math Concepts

1. Introduce the new terms:

   parallelogram A quadrilateral whose opposite sides are parallel and the same length.

   quadrilateral A four-sided polygon.

   rectangle A parallelogram with opposite sides the same length and four right angles.

   rhombus A parallelogram with four equal-length sides.

   square A parallelogram with four equal-length sides and four right angles.

   trapezium A quadrilateral with no parallel sides.

   trapezoid A quadrilateral with one pair of parallel sides.

2. Explore the new terms:
   - The prefix quad means "four." Animals with four legs are called quadrupeds, and sound systems with four separate sound tracks are called quadraphonic.
   - A quadrilateral is a parallelogram only if both pairs of opposite sides are parallel.
   - Parallelograms are any polygons with opposite sides the same length and opposite sides parallel with each other.

- The three special kinds of parallelograms are rectangles, rhombuses, and squares.
- A square is always an example of a rhombus, but a rhombus is not a square because it doesn't have four right angles.
- A square is always an example of a rectangle, but a rectangle is not a square because it does not have four equal sides.
- The diagram below shows these quadrilaterals: trapezium, trapezoid, parallelogram, rhombus, square, and rectangle.

Trapezium

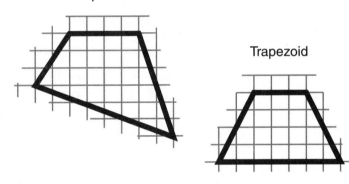

Trapezoid

Parallelogram

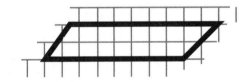

Rhombus

Square

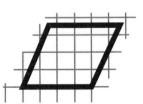

Rectangle

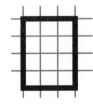

- Squares and rhombuses have congruent sides, which means that all four sides are the same length.
- Another name for parallelogram is rhomboid.

EXTENSIONS

1. Students can compare the properties of parallelograms, rectangles, squares, and rhombuses using the diagrams in the On Your Own problem from Activity 1.

2. Students can use a compass to measure the angles of parallelograms to prove these properties:

   a. Consecutive pairs of angles of a parallelogram are *supplementary* (their sum equals 180°).

   b. Opposite angles of a parallelogram are congruent.

ANSWERS

Activity 1: Quadrilaterals

1. trapezoid
2. trapezium
3. parallelogram (rhombus)
4. parallelogram (square)
5. parallelogram

Activity 2: Parallelograms

1. rhombus
2. square
3. square
4. parallelogram
5. rectangle

19 ACTIVITY 1

Quadrilaterals

A **polygon** is a closed figure formed by three or more line segments that are joined only at the endpoints, with each endpoint connected to only two line segments. A **quadrilateral** is a four-sided polygon. Quadrilaterals can be classified by the number of parallel sides. A **trapezium** is a quadrilateral with no parallel sides. A **trapezoid** is a quadrilateral with one pair of parallel sides. A **parallelogram** is a quadrilateral with two pairs of parallel sides and whose opposite sides are the same length.

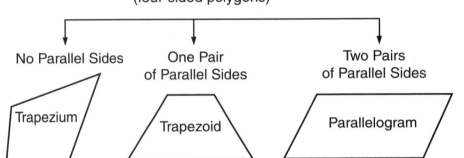

Practice Problems

Study the diagram to answer the following:

1. Which figure is a trapezium?

2. How many of the figures are parallelograms?

3. Which figure is a trapezoid?

1. Think!
- A trapezium has no parallel sides.
- Which figure has no parallel sides?

Answer: Figure F is a trapezium.

2. Think!
- A parallelogram has two pairs of parallel sides.
- Which figures have two pairs of parallel sides? A, B, D, E

Answer: There are four parallelograms.

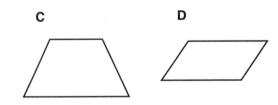
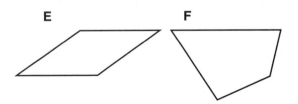

ACTIVITY 1 (continued)

3. Think!

- A trapezoid has one pair of parallel sides.
- Which figure has one pair of parallel sides?

Answer: Figure C is a trapezoid.

On Your Own

Classify the figures below as a trapezium, trapezoid, or parallelogram.

1. _____

2. _____

3. _____

4. _____

5. _____

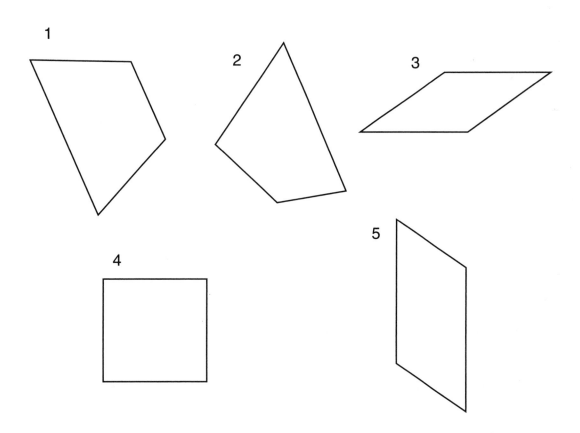

Parallelograms

A parallelogram is a quadrilateral whose opposite sides are parallel and the same length. A small square drawn in the corner of a quadrilateral indicates a right angle. A **rectangle** is a parallelogram with opposite sides the same length and four right angles. A **rhombus** is a parallelogram with four equal-length sides. A **square** is a parallelogram with four equal-length sides and four right angles.

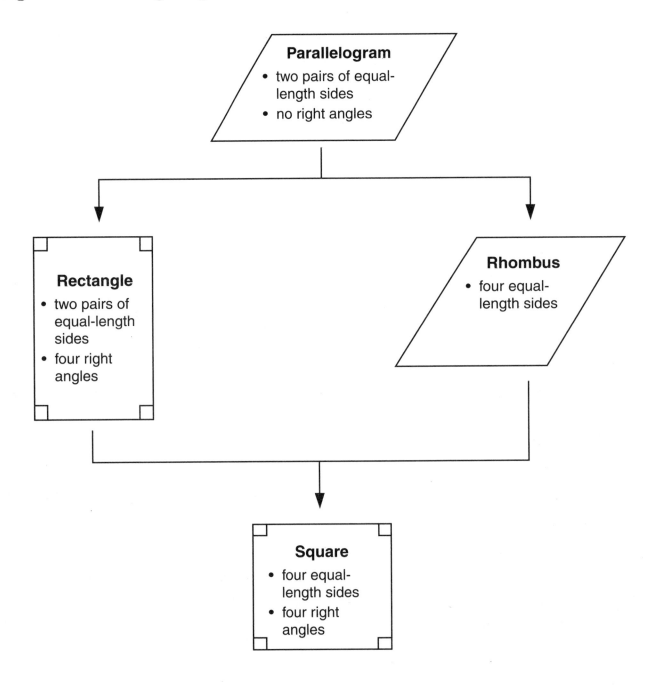

© 2005 by John Wiley & Sons, Inc.

ACTIVITY 2 (continued)

Practice Problems

Write the name that best describes each figure.

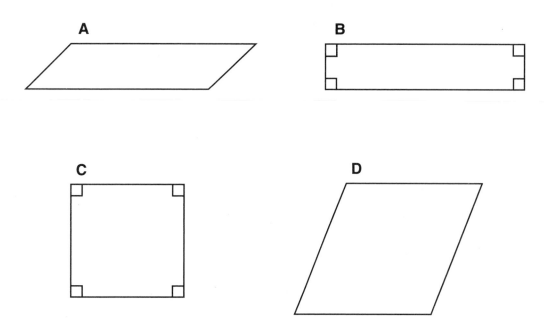

A. Think!

• The figure has two pairs of parallel sides, two pairs of equal-length sides, and no right angles.

Answer: The name that best describes figure A is parallelogram.

B. Think!

• The figure has two pairs of parallel sides, two pairs of equal-length sides, and four right angles.

Answer: The name that best describes figure B is rectangle.

C. Think!

• The figure has two pairs of parallel sides, four equal-length sides, and four right angles.

Answer: The name that best describes figure C is square.

D. Think!

• The figure has two pairs of parallel sides, four equal-length sides, and no right angles.

Answer: The name that best describes figure D is rhombus.

On Your Own

Write the name that best describes each figure below. A ruler can be used to determine the length of the sides of the figures.

1. _____

2. _____

3. _____

4. _____

5. _____

3

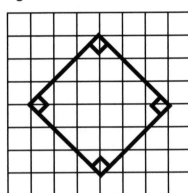

1

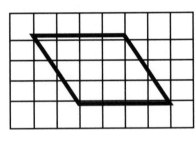

2

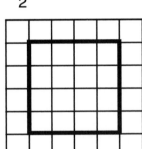

4

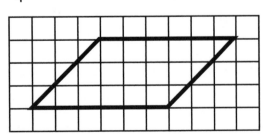

5

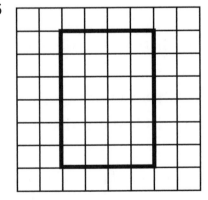

Circles

TEACHING TIPS

Benchmarks

By the end of grade 5, students should be able to
- Measure to solve problems involving circumference.
- Use experimental results to make predictions.

By the end of grade 8, students should be able to
- Describe the relationship between radius, diameter, and circumference of a circle.
- Solve problems involving circumference.

In this chapter, students are expected to
- Measure the diameter and radius of a circle and determine its circumference.
- Determine the value of pi.
- Draw circles of different diameters.

Preparing the Materials

Activity: Exploring Circumferences
- Make a copy of the Exploring Circumferences activity sheet for each student.

Investigation: Pi
- Make a copy of the Pi investigation sheet for each student.
- If empty cans are used, make sure the edges are not sharp. Duct tape can be placed around the edges to make them smooth and safe to touch. Prepare three cans for each student or group. Label the cans A, B, C.

Presenting the Math Concepts

1. Introduce the new terms:

   chord A straight line that begins and ends on a circle.

   circle A plane figure whose points are all the same distance from its center.

   circumference The perimeter of a circle.

   diameter A chord that passes through the center of a circle.

   perimeter The distance around a closed figure.

   pi The ratio of the circumference of a circle to its diameter.

   radius (pl. radii) A line segment from the center of the circle to any point on the circle.

2. Explore the new terms:
   - The circumference of a circle divided by its diameter equals approximately 3.14 or $3\frac{1}{7}$.
   - The ratio of circumference to diameter is equal to pi, which is symbolized by the Greek letter π.
   - Pi is the same for all circles regardless of their size.

EXTENSIONS

1. Circles with different diameters can be used for evaluating understanding of circle terms. Give each student a drawing of two or more circles, and ask them to determine the circles' circumference, diameter, and radius. The measurements can be written on the circles and turned in for evaluation.

2. Students can measure larger or smaller cans than used in the Pi Investigation and compare their circumference-to-diameter ratio. Measurements can be made in English and metric units.

Answers

Activity: Exploring Circumferences

Circle	Circumference, $C = \pi d$	Circumference, $C = 2\pi r$
1. diameter of 3 feet	$C = 3.14 \times 3$ ft $C = 9.42$ ft	$C = 2 \times 3.14 \times 1.5$ ft $C = 9.42$ ft
2. radius of 8 meters	$C = 3.14 \times 16$ m $C = 50.24$ m	$C = 2 \times 3.14 \times 8$ m $C = 50.24$ m
3. diameter of 40 centimeters	$C = 3.14 \times 40$ cm $C = 125.6$ cm	$C = 2 \times 3.14 \times 20$ cm $C = 125.6$ cm
4. radius of 10 yards	$C = 3.14 \times 20$ yds $C = 62.8$ yds	$C = 2 \times 3.14 \times 10$ yds $C = 62.8$ yds

20 ACTIVITY

Exploring Circumferences

A **circle** is a plane figure whose points are all the same distance from its center. A **chord** is a straight line that begins and ends on a circle. The chord that passes through the center of a circle is called the **diameter**. Half the diameter, which is a line segment from the center of the circle to any point on the circle, is called the **radius**. The distance around a closed figure is called its **perimeter**. The perimeter of a circle is called the **circumference**. The formula $C = \pi d$, is read as "circumference equals pi times diameter." **Pi (π)** is the ratio of the circumference of a circle to its diameter, which is equal to approximately 3.14.

Practice Problems

1. Use the formula $C = \pi d$ to find the circumference of the circle in the diagram. Fill in the missing numbers in the equations below.

   $C =$ _____ × _____

   $C =$ _____ inches

   Think!

   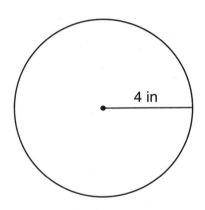
   4 in

   • The radius of the circle is 4 inches. Since the diameter of the circle is two times its radius, the diameter of the circle (d) is 2×4 in = 8 in.

   • Using the value of pi and the diameter of the circle, what is the circumference of the circle?

   Answer: $C = 3.14 \times 8$ in
   $C = 25.12$ inches

2. Use the formula $C = 2\pi r$ to find the circumference of the circle in the diagram. Fill in the missing numbers in the equations below.

   $C = 2 \times$ _____ × _____

   $C =$ _____ cm

   Think!

   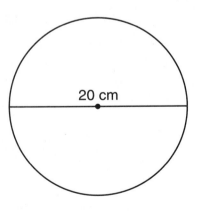
   20 cm

   • The formula $C = 2\pi r$, is read as "circumference equals 2 times pi times radius."

   • The diameter of the circle is 20 cm, so the radius of the circle is 20 cm ÷ 2 = 10 cm.

   • Using the value of pi and the radius of the circle, what is the circumference of the circle?

ACTIVITY (continued)

Answer: $C = 2 \times 3.14 \times 10$ cm

$C = 62.8$ cm

On Your Own

Find the circumference of the circles described in column 1 using the indicated formulas.
Fill in the missing numbers.

Circle	Circumference, $C = \pi d$	Circumference, $C = 2\pi r$
1. diameter of 3 feet	$C = $ _____ $\times$ _____ $C = $ _____	$C = 2 \times$ _____ $\times$ _____ $C = $ _____
2. radius of 8 meters	$C = $ _____ $\times$ _____ $C = $ _____	$C = 2 \times$ _____ $\times$ _____ $C = $ _____
3. diameter of 40 centimeters	$C = $ _____ $\times$ _____ $C = $ _____	$C = 2 \times$ _____ $\times$ _____ $C = $ _____
4. radius of 10 yards	$C = $ _____ $\times$ _____ $C = $ _____	$C = 2 \times$ _____ $\times$ _____ $C = $ _____

20

INVESTIGATION

Pi

PURPOSE

To determine the value of pi.

Materials

metric tape measure
3 different-size cans labeled A, B, C

Procedure

1. Using the tape measure, measure the circumference (distance around) of can A in cm. Record the measurement in the Circumference/Diameter Data table.

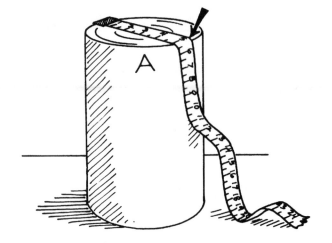

2. Measure the diameter (distance across the top) of can A in cm. Record the measurement in the data table.

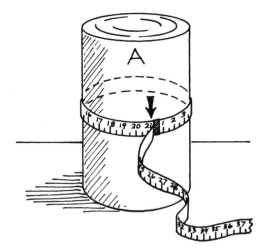

3. Calculate the ratio circumference/diameter for can A by dividing the circumference of the can by its diameter. Record the answer in the data table.

4. Repeat steps 1 through 3 for cans B and C.

5. How does the ratio of circumference/diameter compare for the three cans?

Results

The circumference to diameter ratio for each can should be 3.14. While only three cans are used, it can be assumed that this is true for any size can or round object because $c/d = \pi$.

CIRCUMFERENCE/DIAMETER DATA			
	Measurements		
Object	Circumference (C), cm	Diameter (d), cm	Circumference/Diameter, c/d
A			
B			
C			

21

Areas of Circles

TEACHING TIPS

Benchmarks

By the end of grade 5, students should be able to
- Measure to solve problems involving area.
- Use manipulatives to solve problems.
- Use tools (such as real objects) and technology (such as a calculator) to solve problems.

By the end of grade 8, students should be able to
- Connect models to formulas for solving problems involving surface area.
- Use technological tools and mental math to solve problems.

In this chapter, students are expected to
- Find the area of circles in English and metric units.
- Use a calculator to find answers.
- Model the relationship between the areas of a circle and of a rectangle made from pieces of the circle.

Preparing the Materials

Activity: Area of Circles
- Make a copy of the Area of Circles activity sheet for each student.

Investigation: Rectangle Pie
- Make a copy of the Rectangle Pie Investigation sheet for each student.
- Make a copy of the Pie Pieces sheet for each student.

Presenting the Math Concepts

1. Introduce the new terms:

   area The amount of surface a figure covers.

   power Another name for an exponent.

2. Explore the new terms:
   - In the formula for area of a circle, $A = \pi r^2$,
     (1) The symbol π represents the Greek letter pi, which equals the ratio of the circumference of a circle to its diameter. A decimal approximation for pi is 3.14. A fraction approximation for pi is $3\frac{1}{7}$.
     (2) The variable r^2 doesn't mean $2r$. The 2 is an exponent, and the expression equals $r \times r$.

- The number 4^5 is read as "four raised to the fifth power," or simply "four to the fifth power." This is the same as $4 \times 4 \times 4 \times 4 \times 4$. The second and third powers have special names: 3^2 is "3 to the second power," or "3 squared." 3^3 is "3 to the third power" or "3 cubed."

- When two units are multiplied, such as cm × cm, a small 2 is placed to the upper right of the unit (cm^2), and the combination is read as "square centimeter."

- If a figure is measured in centimeters, its area is expressed in square centimeters (cm^2).

EXTENSION

Students can use the π and x^2 keys on a scientific calculator to find the area of circles. For example, to find the area of a circle with a radius of 4 inches, the calculator keys π and x^2 will be used. Note that scientific calculators vary, but all have two functions for most keys. Pressing the shift key (2nd or Inv are used on some calculators) accesses the second function. On some calculators, π is a second function.

$$A = \pi r^2$$
$$= \pi \times (4 \text{ in})^2$$
$$= 50.24 \text{ in}^2$$

Answers

Activity: Area of Circles

1. **a.** 50.24 in^2
   b. 314.00 cm^2

2. **a.** 50.24 in^2
   b. 314.00 cm^2

3. **a.** 113.04 in^2
   b. 706.50 cm^2

4. **a.** 30.96 in^2
   b. 193.50 cm^2

Area of Circles

Area is the amount of surface a figure covers. The formula for calculating the area of a circle is $A = \pi r^2$, where A = area. The symbol π is read as "pi," which has a value of approximately 3.14, and r = radius. The r is a base number, and the 2 is an exponent. A base number is a number multiplied by itself the number of times equal to the value of the exponent. An exponent, also called a **power**, is a number to the right and above a base number that tells how many times the base is multiplied by itself. In the formula, r^2 is read as "r squared" and means $r \times r$.

Practice Problems

1. Calculate the surface area of the pizza in English units.

   Think!

   - The pizza is a circle.
   - The formula for calculating the area of a circle is $A = \pi r^2$.
   - The radius of the pizza is 6 inches, and π = 3.14.
   - Substitute the values for π and r in the formula:

     $A = 3.14 \times (6 \text{ in})^2$
   - Simplify the exponent: $(6 \text{ in})^2 = 6 \text{ in} \times 6 \text{ in}$. When you multiply 6×6, you get the product 36. When you multiply two units, the product is a square unit.
     So 6 in × 6 in = 36 in², which is read as "36 square inches."

     $A = 3.14 \times 36 \text{ in}^2$

   Answer: $A = 113.04 \text{ in}^2$

2. Calculate the surface of the pizza in metric units.

   Think!

   - Use the radius of 15 cm and the formula $A = \pi r^2$ to determine the area of the pizza in metric units. $A = 3.14 \times (15 \text{ cm})^2$
   - Simplify the exponent. Do this by multiplying 15 cm × 15 cm. Since $15 \times 15 = 225$ and cm × cm = cm², 15 cm × 15 cm = 225 cm².
   - Substitute the value of π and r^2 into the formula and solve for A.

     $A = 3.14 \times 225 \text{ cm}^2$

   Answer: $A = 706.5 \text{ cm}^2$

ACTIVITY (continued)

On Your Own

For each problem, find the area in (a) English and (b) metric measurements. Round each answer to the one-hundredth place.

1. The length of each fan blade from the center of the fan is 4 inches (10 cm). Calculate the area of the circle that the blades sweep with each complete turn.

2. Determine the area of the lid on the can.

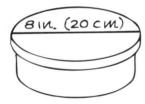

3. The second hand of the clock is 6 inches (15 cm) long. Determine the area that the hand sweeps in 1 minute.

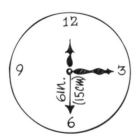

4. A circle was cut from a 12 inch (30 cm) square of material. How much material was not used?

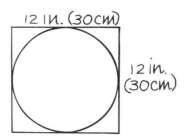

Rectangle Pie

PURPOSE

To compare the area of a circle to the area of a rectangle made with pie pieces from the circle.

Materials

crayon, any color
copy of Pie Pieces diagram
ruler
copy paper
pencil
scissors
transparent tape

Procedure

1. Use the crayon to shade the bottom half of the circle as shown.

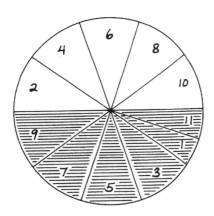

2. Use the ruler to measure the radius of the circle. Using this measurement, determine the product of pi × radius ($\pi \times r$).

3. On the sheet of copy paper, use the ruler and pencil to draw a rectangle with a base equal to the product of the radius × pi and a height equal to the radius of the circle (determined in step 2).

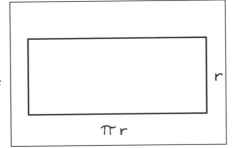

4. Cut out the pie wedges from the circle and arrange them inside the rectangle as shown in the diagram.

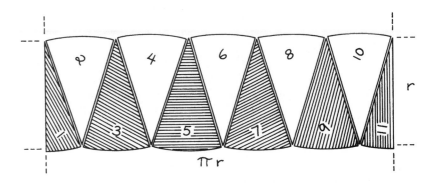

5. Calculate the area of the rectangle using this formula:
$$A = \text{base} \times \text{height}$$
$$= (\pi r)\, r$$

6. Calculate the area of the circle using this formula:
$$A = \pi r^2$$
$$= (\pi r)\, r$$

Results

The pieces from the circle almost fill the rectangle. The area of the rectangle and the area of the circle are the same.

Why?

While there are some empty spaces within the rectangle, some of the pie pieces extend beyond the rectangle. The comparison of the area of the rectangle and the area of the circle indicate that the amount of pie pieces outside the rectangle should equal the empty spaces inside the rectangle. Thus, the area of a circle and the area of a rectangle are the same if the height of the rectangle equals the radius (r) of the circle and the base of the rectangle equals πr.

Pie Pieces

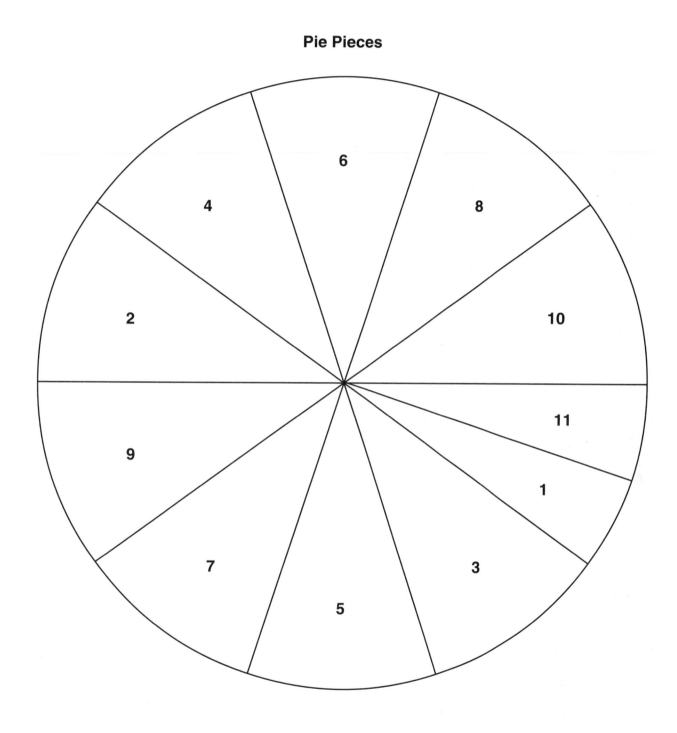

Areas of Parallelograms

TEACHING TIPS

Benchmarks

By the end of grade 5, students should be able to
- Measure to solve problems involving area.
- Use manipulatives to solve problems.

By the end of grade 8, students should be able to
- Connect models to formulas for solving problems involving surface area.

In this chapter, students are expected to
- Calculate the areas of parallelograms and rectangles.
- Use models to compare the areas of parallelograms and rectangles of equal base and height.

Preparing the Materials

Activity: Areas of Parallelograms and Rectangles
- Make a copy of the Areas of Parallelograms and Rectangles activity sheet for each student.

Investigation: Rearrangement
- Make a copy of the Rearrangement investigation sheet for each student.
- Make a copy of the Parallelogram Patterns sheet for each student.

Presenting the Math Concepts

1. Introduce the new terms:

   base On a plane figure, the distance across the bottom.

   height The distance along a plane figure that is perpendicular to the base.

2. Explore the new terms:
   - The symbols for area, base, and height respectively are *A, b, h.*
   - Area is usually measured by the number of equal-size squares that fit into a figure.
   - Since a formula is an equation, the two parts on opposite sides of the equal sign have the same value.
   - The area of a rectangle is determined by the formula
     area = base × height
     $A = b \times h$
   - Two variables written together (such as *bh*) indicates that they are multiplied by each other.

- The area of a parallelogram is determined by the same equation as for a rectangle, $A = b \times h$. The difference is that the height in this equation is not the parallelogram's slanted side, but rather a perpendicular measurement from its base. In diagrams, the height of a parallelogram is usually shown as a dashed line.
- The area of a parallelogram is the same as that of a rectangle of equal base and height.
- A figure without a specific unit measurement label is measured simply in units. Each square on a grid is 1 unit. The area of a figure on a grid would be measured in units[2].

EXTENSIONS

1. Give students an area of a figure and ask them to find as many height/base pairs as possible. For example, for a rectangle with an area of 100 ft[2], the possible height/base pairs include 10 ft × 10 ft and 2 ft × 50 ft.

2. Students can find missing measurements. Give them problems with one of the three variables in the area formula missing. You may wish to have them show the steps for determining the answer. For example:

   Problem:
   Area = 25 ft[2]
   base = 5 ft
   height = ?

   Answer:
   $$A = b \times h$$
   $$25 \text{ ft}^2 = 5 \text{ ft} \times h$$
   $$25 \text{ ft}^2 \div 5 \text{ ft} = 5 \text{ ft} \times h \div 5 \text{ ft}$$
   $$h = 5 \text{ ft}$$

ANSWERS

Activity: Areas of Parallelograms and Rectangles

Problem	Formula	Calculation	Answer
1	$A = b \times h$	$A = 5.5 \text{ ft} \times 4 \text{ ft}$	$A = 22 \text{ ft}^2$
2	$A = b \times h$	$A = 456 \text{ km} \times 589 \text{ km}$	$A = 268{,}584 \text{ km}^2$
3	$A = b \times h$	$A = 5 \text{ units} \times 2 \text{ units}$	$A = 10 \text{ units}^2$

© 2005 by John Wiley & Sons, Inc.

ACTIVITY

Areas of Parallelograms and Rectangles

On a plane figure, such as a parallelogram, the **base** is the distance across the bottom. The **height** is the distance perpendicular to its base. The formula for finding the area of a rectangle is area = base × height ($A = b \times h$). The area of a parallelogram is found using the same formula, but the height of a parallelogram is a perpendicular line from the base. In the figure, the height is shown as a dashed line, but any vertical line from the base could be used to determine the height.

Parallelogram

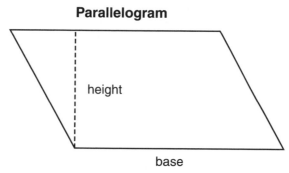

height

base

Practice Problems

Find the areas of figures A and B.

A. Think!

- Figure A is a rectangle.

- The term *unit* is used as a measure when a figure is without specific unit measurement, such as inches or centimeters. Each square on this grid is 1 unit.

- The base of the rectangle is the bottom distance, which is 6 units.

- The height of the rectangle is the vertical distance, which is 5 units.

- The formula for finding the area of the rectangle is $A = b \times h = 6$ units × 5 units.

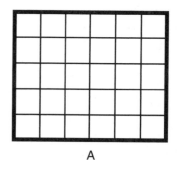

A

Answer: 30 units^2

B. Think!

- Figure B is a parallelogram.

- The base of the parallelogram is 6 units.

- The height of the parallelogram shown by the dashed line is 3 units.

- The formula for finding the area of the parallelogram is $A = b \times h = 6$ units × 3 units.

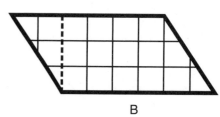

B

Answer: 18 units^2

© 2005 by John Wiley & Sons, Inc.

Janice VanCleave's Teaching the Fun of Math **127**

On Your Own

For the following, show the formula and the calculations used for solving the problem.

1. The surface of the desk is a rectangle. Find the surface area of the desk.

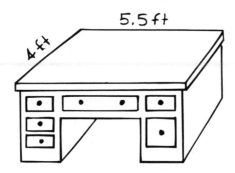

5.5 ft

4 ft

2. Colorado is nearly rectangular. Determine its approximate area.

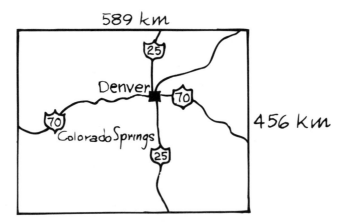

589 km

Denver

Colorado Springs

456 km

3. Find the area of the parallelogram that forms the body of the dog.

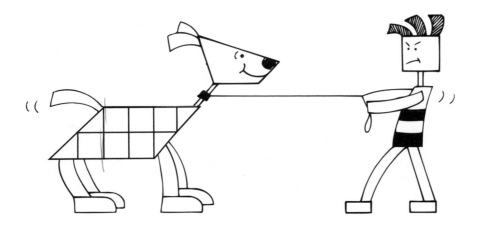

Rearrangement

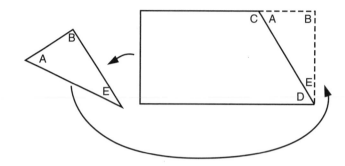

PURPOSE

To compare the areas of a parallelogram and a rectangle.

Materials

copy of Parallelogram Patterns sheet
scissors
stick glue
sheet of copy paper

Procedure

1. In the Parallelogram Area Data table, record the number of squares of the base (line ED) and height (line BE) of parallelogram A from the Parallelogram Patterns sheet.

2. Calculate the area of the parallelogram using the value of the base and height from step 1 and the following equation. Record the area in the table.

$$A_{(parallelogram)} = base \times height$$

3. Cut out parallelogram A. Then cut along the dashed height line BE. Two pieces will be formed, one a triangle and the other a trapezoid.

4. Glue the trapezoid to the copy paper.

5. Glue the triangle to the paper so that line AE on the triangle and line CD on the trapezoid match up. Note that a rectangle has been formed.

6. Record the number of squares of the base (line ED) and height (line BE) of the new rectangle you formed.

7. Calculate the area of the rectangle using the value of the base and height from step 6 and the following equation. Record the area in the table.

$$A_{(rectangle)} = base \times height$$

8. Repeat steps 1 through 7 for parallelogram B.

9. How does the area each parallelogram compare to the area of the corresponding rectangle formed from its pieces?

Results

The base and height of the parallelogram are equal to the base and height of the rectangle formed. A parallelogram has the same area as a rectangle of equal base and height.

PARALLELOGRAM AREA DATA						
Parallelogram				**Rectangle**		
Figure	**Base**	**Height**	**Area**	**Base**	**Height**	**Area**
A						
B						

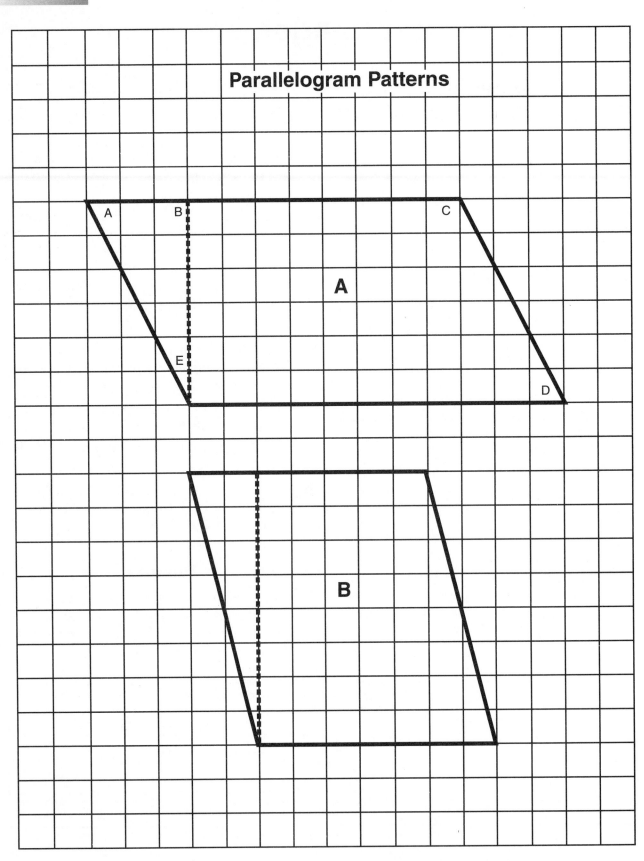

Parallelogram Patterns

A

B

Areas of Triangles

TEACHING TIPS

Benchmarks

By the end of grade 5, students should be able to
• Measure to solve problems involving area.
• Use manipulatives to solve problems.

By the end of grade 8, students should be able to
• Connect models to formulas for solving problems involving surface area.

In this chapter, students are expected to
• Calculate the areas of triangles.
• Use models to determine the formula for the areas of triangles.

Preparing the Materials

Activity: Areas of Triangles
• Make a copy of the Areas of Triangles activity sheet for each student.

Investigation: Half as Much
• Make a copy of the Half as Much investigation sheet for each student.
• Give each student 2 unlined white index cards.
• Make sure each student has 2 different-colored crayons and tape.

Presenting the Math Concepts

1. Introduce the new term:
   adjacent Adjoining sides.

2. Explore the new term:
   • A triangle has half the area of a rectangle of equal base and height.
   • The area of a right triangle is equal to ½ the product of the adjacent sides of the right angle. In other words, the base and height are adjacent sides that form a right angle (90° angle).
   • The formula for finding the area of any triangle is $A = ½ (b \times h)$.
   • When solving for area, find the product inside the parenthesis first. Then multiply the product by ½. Multiplying by ½ is the same as dividing by 2.
   • In a triangle without a right angle, the height is a perpendicular line segment from the base to one of the vertices.

EXTENSION

The height of some triangles is determined by a line segment outside the triangle. Make a sheet of triangles for which the height is determined by a line segment outside the triangle and ask students to find the area of each triangle.

ANSWERS

Activity: Area of Triangles

1. 75 in^2
2. 16 m^2

Areas of Triangles

The area of a triangle is determined by the equation $A = ½$ (base × height), or $A = ½ (b × h)$. In a right triangle, the base and height are **adjacent** (adjoining sides) sides that form the right angle. In other triangles, any side can be designated as the base, and the height is a line segment perpendicular to that base that connects with one of the triangle's vertices (the point where two sides meet).

Practice Problems

Find the areas of triangles A and B.

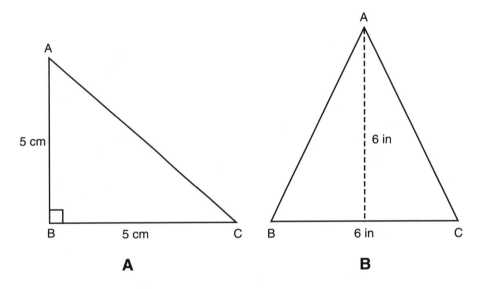

A   **B**

A. Think!

- Triangle A is a right triangle, so the base and height are adjacent sides that form the right angle.
- The base of the triangle, line segment BC, equals 5 cm.
- The height of the triangle, line segment AB, equals 5 cm.
- Using the formula for area: $A = ½ (b × h) = ½$ (5 cm × 5 cm)
- Multiply the numbers and units in the parenthesis first, then multiply by ½ (which is the same as dividing by 2).
- $A = ½$ (5 cm × 5 cm)
  $= ½$ (25 cm²)

Answer: 12.5 cm²

ACTIVITY (continued)

B. Think!

- Triangle B is not a right triangle, so one of the sides, generally the bottom or horizontal, is randomly identified as the base, and the height is a perpendicular line segment from that base to a vertex. This is shown by a dashed line in the diagram.
- The base of the triangle is 6 inches.
- The height of the triangle is 6 inches.
- Using the formula for area:

$A = \frac{1}{2} (b \times h)$

$A = \frac{1}{2} (6 \text{ in} \times 6 \text{ in})$

$\quad = \frac{1}{2} (36 \text{ in}^2)$

Answer: 18 in^2

On Your Own

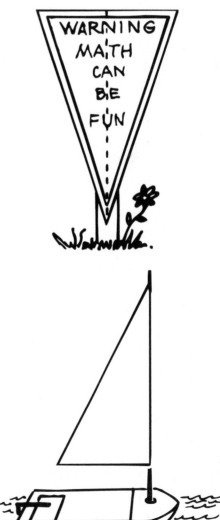

1. Find the area of the sign if it has a base of 10 inches and a height of 15 inches.

2. Find the area of the sail if it has a base of 4 m and a height of 8 m. (Note: The sail is a right triangle.)

Half as Much

PURPOSE

To demonstrate the relationship between the area of a rectangle and the area of a triangle.

Materials

pencil
ruler
2 white, unlined index cards
2 crayons of different colors
scissors
transparent tape

Procedure

1. Use the pencil and ruler to draw a diagonal line across one of the index cards. Two triangles will be formed.

2. Use a crayon to color one of the triangles on the card.

3. Use the scissors to cut along the diagonal line that separates the two triangles.

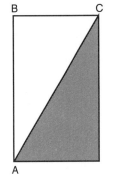

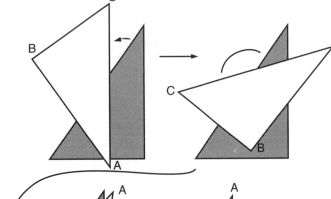

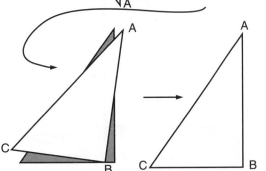

4. Place the two pieces together to form the original rectangle. Then rotate the white triangle 180° so that it covers the colored triangle. Compare the shapes and sizes of the two overlapping triangles.

5. Use the ruler and pencil to make a dot along the center of one of the short sides of the second index card.

6. With the ruler and pencil, draw two lines from the dot to the corners on the opposite side of the card. Use the remaining crayon to color the center triangle that is formed.

7. Cut out the colored triangle.

8. Place sides AB of the two remaining uncolored triangles together and secure the pieces with tape.

9. Place the triangle formed by the taped pieces over the colored triangle. Compare the shapes and sizes of the two overlapping triangles.

Results

Two identical triangles are formed from each card.

Why?

The base and height of each triangle formed is equal to the base and height of the rectangular card each is formed from. Since a triangle has half the area of a rectangle of equal base and height, two triangles of equal area can be formed from each card.

Volume

TEACHING TIPS

Benchmarks

By the end of grade 5, students should be able to
- Estimate and measure capacity.
- Use models to compare capacity.

By the end of grade 8, students should be able to
- Use appropriate units, tools, or formulas to measure and to solve problems involving capacity.
- Use a table of data.

In this chapter, students are expected to
- Measure the solid and liquid volume of a box.

Preparing the Materials

Activity: Solid Volume
- Make a copy of the Solid Volume activity sheet for each student.

Investigation: Full Up
- Make a copy of the Full Up investigation sheet for each student.
- Provide each student with a 30-by-30-cm piece of white poster board.
- Use a plastic shoebox to catch any spills.
- Provide each student with school glue, markers, and a 500-mL measuring cup.

Presenting the Math Concepts

1. Introduce the new terms:

   height For solid figures, it is the distance perpendicular to the base of the figure.

   length For solid figures, it is the longest base distance.

   polyhedron A solid whose faces are polygons.

   solid figure A figure that has three dimensions and volume.

   three-dimensional (3-D) Having three measurements—length, width, height; said of solid figures.

   width For solid figures, it is the shortest base distance.

2. Explore the new terms:
   - The volume of a solid is the number of cubic units it contains. A cubic unit is the product of three units, such as cm × cm × cm = cm³.
   - Solids are 3-D figures, which means they have length, width, and height. Generally, for a solid figure the longest measure of the base is its length and the shortest measure of its base is its width. Its height is the vertical measure perpendicular to the base. But since rotating the figure would change the order of its measurement, in calculating the volume of the figure it doesn't matter which side is labeled length, width, or height. Changing the position of a solid doesn't change the three measurements that are multiplied together. Likewise, the order in which the numbers are multiplied does not change the product.
   - The formula for calculating the volume of polyhedrons using length measurement is $V = $ length $\times$ width $\times$ height, or $V = L \times W \times H$. For example, a box with a length of 5 cm, width of 9 cm, and height of 10 cm would have a volume of 5 cm $\times$ 9 cm $\times$ 10 cm = 450 cm³.
   - One mL is the same volume as 1 cm³.

EXTENSION

Students can use the Full Up investigation to prove that 1 cm³ equals 1 mL.

ANSWERS

Activity: Solid Volume

1. 80 m³

2. English: 1,800 in³; metric: 28,500 cm³

3. The volume of the aquarium is 62,730 cm³. Volume of 25 pitchers = 50,000 cm³. No, 25 pitchers will not fill the aquarium.

24 ACTIVITY

Solid Volume

Three-dimensional (3-D) is anything that has three measurements—length, width, and height—such as a box. A **solid figure** is a figure that has volume and three dimensions—**length** equal to the longest measure of the base, **width** equal to the shortest measure of the base, and **height** equal to the measure perpendicular to the base. Volume is the amount of space taken up by an object or enclosed by the object; it is the amount a container can hold. The volume of a **polyhedron**, which is a solid whose faces are polygons, is determined by the formula V = length × width × height, or $V = L \times W \times H$.

The horizontal measure of a box is generally called its length, the depth of a box its width, and the vertical measure its height. When multiplying three units together, the product is a cubic unit. So the volume of polyhedrons is measured in cubic units.

Practice Problem

How do the volumes of boxes A, B, and C compare?

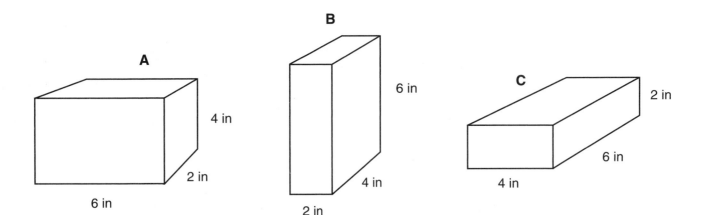

Think!

- Use the formula $V = L \times W \times H$ to calculate the volume of box A. When you multiply the numbers together $(6 \times 2 \times 4)$, you get 48. When you multiply three units, the product is a cube unit. So,

  $V = 6$ in $\times 2$ in $\times 4$ in $= 48$ in^3, which is read as "48 cubic inches."

- Use the formula to calculate the volume of box B.

  $V = 2$ in $\times 4$ in $\times 6$ in $= 48$ in^3

- Use the formula to calculate the volume of box C.

  $V = 4$ in $\times 6$ in $\times 2$ in $= 48$ in^3

Answer: The volumes of all three boxes are the same.

ACTIVITY (continued)

24

On Your Own

1. What is the volume of the room? _____

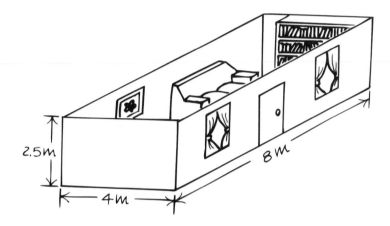

2. Calculate the volume of the picnic cooler in English and metric units. _____

_____

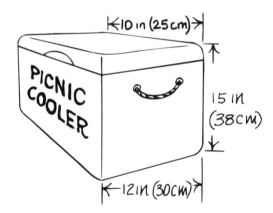

3. If a pitcher holding 2,000 cm³ of water is used to fill an aquarium that is 51 cm wide, 30 cm long, and 41 cm deep, would 25 pitchers of water fill it? _____

Full Up

PURPOSE

To compare the volume units of mL and cm³.

Materials

pen
metric ruler
30-by-30-cm piece of white poster board
marker
school glue
plastic shoebox
500-mL measuring cup
tap water

Procedure

1. Use the pen and ruler to divide the poster board into 1-cm squares.

2. With the marker and ruler, make the darker solid and dashed lines as shown.

3. Turn the paper over and fold it along one of the dark lines. Unfold the paper and repeat, folding along each of the four dark lines.

4. Cut along the dashed lines.

5. Fold sides A and D toward the center, then glue tab A to the back of side A. Be sure to cover the seams with glue.

6. Fold side B toward the center, then glue tab B to the back of side B. Continue folding and gluing until the box is formed.

7. Allow the glue to dry. Then set the paper box into the plastic shoebox.

8. Fill the cup to the 500-mL mark with water. Slowly pour the water into the box.

9. Repeat step 8.

Results

One thousand mL of water fills the box.

Why?

The volume of a box is measured by multiplying its length by its width by its height. The box is 10 cm on each side, so its volume is 1,000 cm³ (10 cm × 10 cm × 10 cm). Volume is also measured in liters or portions of liters. One mL is the same volume as 1 cm³. This means that 1,000 cm³ is the same as 1,000 mL. Since 1,000 mL equals 1 liter, the box can be said to have a volume of 1 liter.

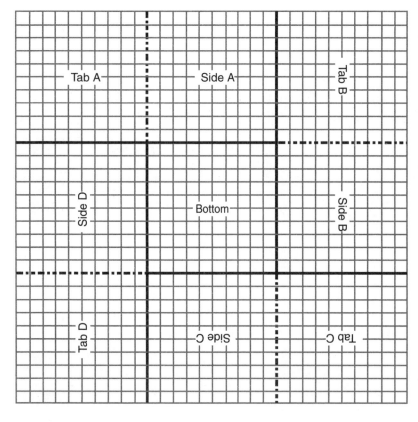

Legend: ——— fold   ▪▪▪▪▪ fold and cut

© 2005 by John Wiley & Sons, Inc.

Reflection and Line Symmetry

TEACHING TIPS

Benchmarks

By the end of grade 5, students should be able to
- Demonstrate reflection using models.
- Use reflection to verify that two shapes are congruent.
- Use reflection to verify that a shape has symmetry.

By the end of grade 8, students should be able to
- Describe the transformation that generates one figure from the other when using two congruent figures.

In this chapter, students are expected to
- Make predictions about reflections and make models to check predictions.
- Make a model showing lines of symmetry.

Preparing the Materials

Activity: Reflections and Lines of Symmetry
- Make a copy of the Reflections and Lines of Symmetry activity sheet for each student.
- Make 7 squares of copy paper about 3 inches (7.5 cm) square for each student.

Investigation: Flaky
- Make a copy of the Flaky investigation sheet for each student.
- Make sure the students have a drawing compass and a protractor.

Presenting the Math Concepts

1. Introduce the new terms:

   flip To turn a plane figure over.

   line of symmetry A line along which a figure can be folded into congruent halves.

   reflection The mirror image of a figure that has been flipped over a line.

   symmetric figure A figure that has one or more lines of symmetry.

2. Explore the new terms:
   - A line of symmetry divides a figure into two identical parts that are mirror images of each other, meaning that if a mirror is placed on the line, a whole figure can be seen. The image in the mirror is the reflected or flipped image, with the right to left being reversed.

- If a figure is folded along the line of symmetry, the two halves will exactly match.
- A reflection is an image that has been flipped over a real or imaginary line.
- A reflection is the same size and shape as the original figure but is a mirror image; it is reversed from right to left.

EXTENSION

Letters such as C, D, E, I, O, and X have a line of symmetry from left to right. These letters can be flipped over a horizontal line of symmetry as shown and still look the same.

--C-D-E-I-O--   line of symetry

Students can discover which letters have a line of symmetry from top to bottom. These letters, such as A, can be flipped over a vertical line of symmetry and still look the same.

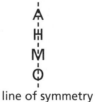

line of symmetry

ANSWERS

Activity: Reflections and Lines of Symmetry

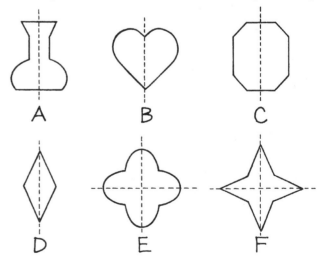

25 ACTIVITY

Reflections and Lines of Symmetry

A **reflection** is the mirror image of a figure that has been flipped over a line. **Flip** means to turn a plane figure over. For the diagram, figure B is a reflection of figure A. Figure B is a flipped version of figure A.

A **symmetric figure**, such as the tree in the diagram, has one or more lines of symmetry. A **line of symmetry** is a line along which a figure can be folded into congruent halves. For the tree diagram, line AB is not a line of symmetry, but line CD is.

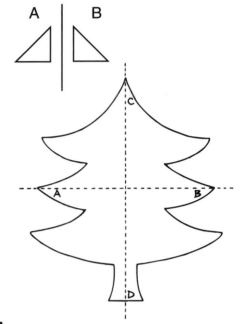

Practice Problems

1. In the figure, half of a polygon is drawn on the fold of a sheet of paper. Predict the shape of the polygon if it is cut out and the paper is unfolded.

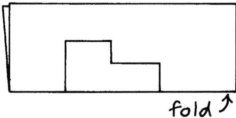

Think!

- The fold is a line of symmetry.
- The shapes of the figure on either side of the fold are reflections or mirror images of each other. This means that one figure has been flipped over a line.
- Imagine the fold as a line with a reflection of the figure over the line.

Answer: The figure below shows an example of a prediction for the reflection.

2. How does your prediction compare to an actual cut-out figure?

Think!

- Fold a sheet of paper in half.
- Draw half of a polygon along the fold.
- Cut out the half of the polygon, cutting through both sheets but not cutting the folded side.
- Unfold the cut-out piece.

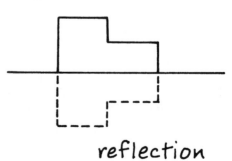

• Compare the cut-out with the drawing for your prediction. How do the predicted shape and the cut-out shape compare?

Answer: The predicted diagram and cut-out are congruent.

On Your Own

1. Figures A through D are drawn on paper folded in half. Make a prediction of how each figure would appear when unfolded. In the Reflection and Line Symmetry Data table, make a diagram of your prediction.

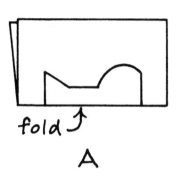

A

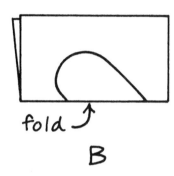

B

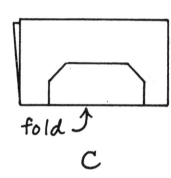

C

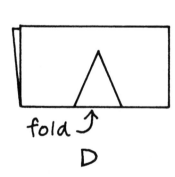

D

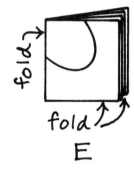

E

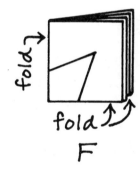

F

25

ACTIVITY (continued)

		Comparison of Prediction and Cut-out	
Shape	Diagram of Predicted Shape	Congruent	Not Congruent
A			
B			
C			
D			
E			
F			

REFLECTION AND LINE SYMMETRY DATA

2. Check your predictions for figures A, B, C, and D following step 2 from the practice problems. In the table, record whether the cut-out and your prediction are congruent.

3. Figures E and F are drawn on paper that has been folded in half twice. Make a prediction of how each figure would appear when unfolded. In the Reflection and Line Symmetry Data table, make a diagram of your prediction.

4. Check your predictions for figures E and F.
   - Repeat step 2 using a sheet of paper that has been folded in half twice, once from top to bottom and then from side to side.

Flaky

PURPOSE

To create a figure with 6 sides and 12 lines of symmetry.

Materials

drawing compass
copy paper
pencil
protractor
ruler
scissors

Procedure

1. Use the compass to draw an 8-inch (20-cm) diameter circle on the paper.

2. Use the pencil to make a dot in the center of the circle, which is where the point of the compass makes a tiny hole.

3. Cut out the circle.

4. Fold the paper circle in half.

5. Use the protractor and pencil to mark a 60° angle and a 120° angle from the center point of the fold line on the folded circle.

6. With the pencil and ruler, draw dashed lines for the two angles as shown.

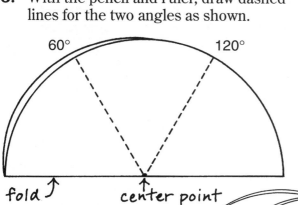

7. Fold the paper forward along one of the dashed lines and backward along the other.

8. Fold the cone-shaped paper in half by placing the straight sides together.

9. Cut a piece out of the rounded side as shown. Then cut two triangular notches in each side and cut off the pointed end.

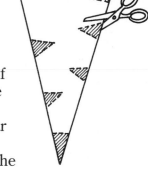

10. Unfold the paper.

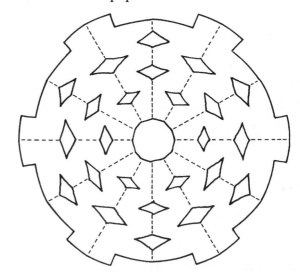

Results

A lacy 6-sided snowflake pattern is produced. The snowflake has 12 lines of symmetry.

Why?

The multiple folding of the paper produces 12 layers of paper with 12 folded edges. The notches cut along the rounded edge and across the folded edges produce a pattern with 6 sides, with each being a line of symmetry. Lines midway between each side are also lines of symmetry, so the pattern has 12 lines of symmetry.

Rotational Symmetry

TEACHING TIPS

Benchmarks

By the end of grade 5, students should be able to
- Demonstrate rotation using models.
- Verify that a shape has rotational symmetry.

By the end of grade 8, students should be able to
- Communicate mathematical ideas using mathematical models.
- Make conjectures from patterns.

In this chapter, students are expected to
- Determine if figures have rotational symmetry, and if so, the fractional turn that rotates the figure onto itself.
- Use a model to determine the rotational symmetry of a figure.

Preparing the Materials

Activity: Rotational Symmetry
- Make a copy of the Rotational Symmetry activity sheet for each student.

Investigation: Turn Around
- Make a copy of the Turn Around investigation sheet for each student.
- Cut one 6-inch (15-cm) square of corrugated cardboard for each student.
- Red and blue crayons are listed among the materials, but any two colors will work.

Presenting the Math Concepts

1. Introduce the new terms:

    clockwise Rotation in the direction of the hands of a clock as viewed from the front or above.

    counterclockwise Rotation in the opposite direction of the hands of a clock as viewed from the front or above.

    point symmetry Characteristic of a figure if it looks unchanged after a 180° rotation.

    rotation A transformation that turns a figure around a point.

    rotational symmetry Characteristic of a figure if it looks unchanged after a rotation of less than 360°.

transformation A change in the position or size of a figure.

2. Explore the new terms:
- Rotation is a transformation that turns a figure around a point. A full turn is a 360° rotation, a one-fourth turn is a 90° rotation, a one-half turn is a 180° rotation, and a three-fourths turn is a 270° rotation.
- A figure has rotational symmetry if a rotation of less than 360° rotates the figure onto itself.
- A figure has point symmetry if a rotation of 180° rotates the figure onto itself.
- The shape of a figure does not change as it is rotated.

EXTENSION

Diagrams of objects with parts that are equal angles apart can be used to demonstrate rotational symmetry. Do this by laying two cut-outs of the same figure together. Rotate the top figure and determine if the figure rotates onto itself.

ANSWERS

Activity: Rotational Symmetry

ROTATIONAL SYMMETRY DATA		
Question	Figure	Rotational Symmetry
1.	A	½ turn
	B	¼, ½, and ¾ turns
	C	½ turn
	D	none
2.	E	360°
	F	90°
	G	360°

Rotational Symmetry

Transformation is a change in the position or size of a figure. **Rotation** is a transformation that turns a figure around a point. A figure has **point symmetry** if it looks unchanged after a 180° rotation. A figure has **rotational symmetry** if it looks unchanged after a rotation of less than 360°. When viewing a figure from the front or above, if it turns in the same direction as the hands of a clock, it is said to turn **clockwise.** If it turns in the opposite direction of clock hands when viewed from the front or above, it is said to turn **counterclockwise.**

Practice Problems

1. Decide whether the figure has rotational symmetry. If it does, name the clockwise fractional turn that rotates the figure onto itself.

Think!

- The figure is a parallelogram.
- Imagine the parallelogram turning about a point through its center. Note: The star is added so you can determine how far the figure has turned.
- The parallelogram overlaps itself at one-half turn only.
- One-half turn is equal to 180°.

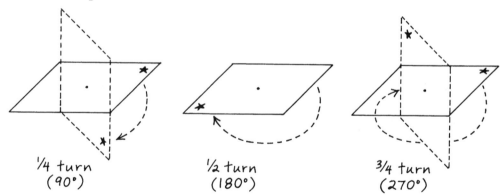

¼ turn
(90°)   ½ turn
(180°)   ¾ turn
(270°)

Answer: The figure has half-turn (180°) rotational symmetry.

2. Does the figure of the ice cream cone have rotational symmetry? What is the least rotation that will land the ice cream cone on top of itself?

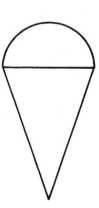

Think!

- The ice cream cone has to make one full turn before it lands on top of itself.

Answer: The figure of the ice cream cone does not have rotational symmetry. It has to rotate (turn) 360° to land on top of itself.

On Your Own

1. Decide if any of the figures A, B, C, or D have rotational symmetry. If they do, name the clockwise fractional turns that rotate the figures onto themselves, and record them in the Rotational Symmetry Data table.

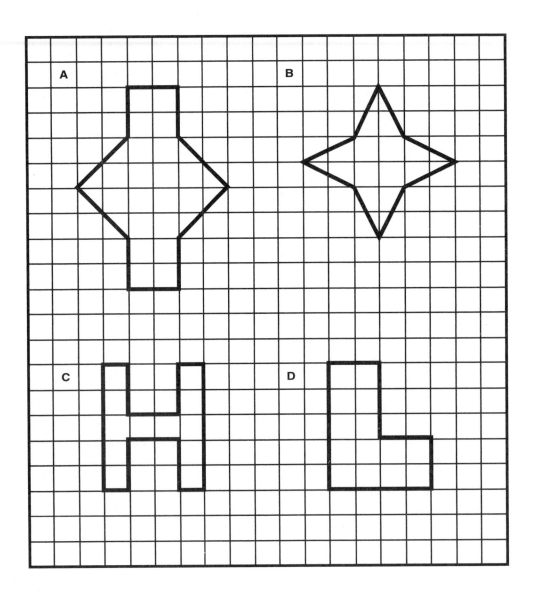

2. What is the least rotation that will land figures E, F, and G on top of themselves? Record the answers in degrees in the table.

ACTIVITY (continued)

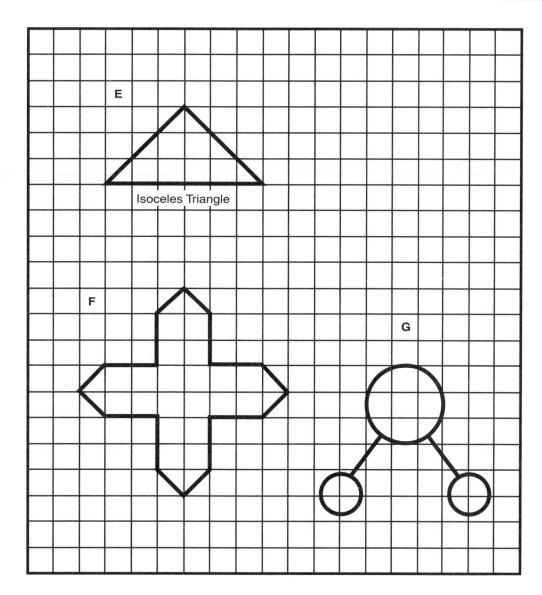

E

Isoceles Triangle

F

G

ROTATIONAL SYMMETRY DATA		
Question	**Figure**	**Rotational Symmetry**
1.	A	
	B	
	C	
	D	
2.	E	
	F	
	G	

26

INVESTIGATION

Turn Around

PURPOSE

To determine the degree of rotational symmetry for a square.

Materials

scissors
2 squares of grid paper, one 12-by-12 cm,
    one 4-by-4 cm
transparent tape
15-by-15-cm piece of corrugated cardboard
2 crayons: 1 red, 1 blue
pushpin

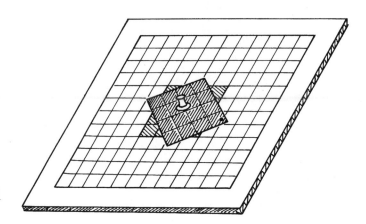

Procedure

1. Tape the 12-by-12-cm square of grid paper in the center of the piece of corrugated cardboard.

2. In the center of the grid paper taped to the cardboard color a 4-by-4-cm square red.

3. Color the remaining 4-by-4-cm-square grid paper blue. Lay the blue square over the red square.

4. Insert the pushpin through the center of the squares and into the cardboard.

5. Use the red crayon to make a dot on the upper right corner of the top, blue square.

6. Rotate the blue square clockwise until it overlaps the red square. Continue to turn the blue square, counting how many times it overlaps the red square before it returns to its starting position. (Do not count the overlapping when it is at its starting point.)

Results

The squares overlap three times.

Why?

As the blue square rotates, it overlaps the red square at one-fourth, one-half, and three-fourths of a turn. Thus the square has $90°$, $180°$, and $270°$ rotational symmetry.

Solid Figures

TEACHING TIPS

Benchmarks

By the end of grade 5, students should be able to
- Describe shapes and solids in terms of vertices, edges, and faces.

By the end of grade 8, students should be able to
- Communicate mathematical ideas using mathematical models.

In this chapter, students are expected to
- Identify polyhedron and non-polyhedron solid figures.
- Use a net to prepare a model of a solid figure.
- Prepare a model of a rectangular pyramid.

Preparing the Materials

Activity 1: Solids
- Make a copy of the Solids activity sheet for each student.

Activity 2: Nets
- Make a copy of the Nets activity sheet for each student.
- Make one copy each of Nets-1 and Nets-2 for each student.
- Provide students with scissors and transparent tape to make the models.

Presenting the Math Concepts

1. Introduce the new terms:

base The bottom of a solid figure; the parallel faces of a prism or cylinder.

cone A solid figure that has curved sides and one circular base.

cube A rectangular prism whose faces are six congruent squares; a square prism.

cylinder A solid figure that has curved sides and two congruent circular bases.

edge A line segment where two faces of a solid figure come together.

face A flat surface of a solid.

net A flat pattern that can be folded into a solid figure.

prism A solid figure with polygonal faces and two congruent parallel bases.

pyramid A solid figure whose base is a polygon and whose faces are triangles with a common vertex.

rectangular prism A solid figure whose six faces are all rectangular.

sphere A solid figure with no flat bases and with all points on its curved surface an equal distance from its center.

vertex The point where two or more edges of a solid figure meet.

2. Explore the new terms:
- A solid figure takes up space.
- A cone is shaped like an ice cream cone—without the scoop of ice cream.
- A cylinder is shaped like a can.
- A sphere is shaped like a ball.
- Polygons are made up of line segments. So polyhedrons, which are solids with polygon faces, are also made up of line segments.
- A box is a rectangular prism.
- The flat side that a solid figure sits on is its base. This can be the bottom of a cone or a cylinder, for example. Note that the two parallel sides of a prism are its bases. A sphere doesn't have a base.

EXTENSIONS

1. Students can make nets for other solid figures such as a rectangular prism and a rectangular pyramid.
2. Students can use straws to construct other solid figures, such as a cube, a rectangular prism, a triangular pyramid, and a rectangular pyramid.

ANSWERS

Activity 1: Solids

1. 1 (E)

2. 1 (B)

3. 2 (B and E)

4. 4 (B, C, D, and E)

5. 3 (B, C, and E)

6. E

7. B

8. They all have curved sides.

9. They both have curved sides and at least one base.

10. Figure C has a vertex, and Figure D has two congruent bases.

Activity 2: Nets

1. a. triangular pyramid

   b. cube

ACTIVITY 1

Solids

A solid figure is a three-dimensional figure. Three-dimensional (3-D) figures have three measurements—length, width, and height. The bottom of a solid figure is its **base**. The flat surface of a solid is called a **face**. The line segment where two faces of a solid come together is called an **edge**. The point where two or more edges of a solid figure meet is called a **vertex**. The solid figures are the **cone** (a solid figure that has curved sides and one circular base), the **cube** (a rectangular prism whose faces are six congruent squares), the **cylinder** (a solid figure that has curved sides and two congruent circular bases), the polyhedron (a solid figure whose faces are polygons), the **prism** (a solid figure with polygonal faces and two congruent parallel bases), the **pyramid** (a solid figure whose base is a polygon and whose faces are triangles with a common vertex), the **rectangular prism** (a solid figure whose six faces are all rectangular), and the **sphere** (a solid figure with no flat bases and with all points on its curved surface an equal distance from its center).

Practice Problems

Identify solid figures A, B, C, D, and E in the drawing.

A. Think!

- Figure A, the hat, has curved sides and one circular base.
- A solid that has curved sides and one circular base is a cone.

Answer: Figure A is a cone.

B. Think!

- Figure B, the ball, is curved on all sides with no flat bases and with all points on its curved surface an equal distance from its center.
- A solid figure with no flat bases and with all points on its curved surface an equal distance from its center is called a sphere.

Answer: Figure B is a sphere.

C. Think!

- Figure C is a pyramid with a rectangular base.
- A solid figure that is a pyramid with a rectangular base is a rectangular pyramid.

Answer: Figure C is a rectangular pyramid.

D. Think!
- Figure D, the cookie box, has six faces that are all rectangular.
- A solid figure with six faces that are all rectangular is a rectangular prism.

Answer: Figure D is a rectangular prism.

E. Think!
- Figure E, the soup can, has curved sides and two congruent circular bases.
- A solid figure that has curved sides and two congruent circular bases is a cylinder.

Answer: Figure E is a cylinder.

On Your Own

Study figures A, B, C, D, and E below to answer the following questions.

A   B   C   D   E

1. How many prisms are represented? _____

2. How many pyramids are represented? _____

3. How many of the figures are polyhedrons? _____

4. How many of the figures have bases? _____

5. How many of the figures have vertices? _____

6. Which figure is a rectangular prism? _____

7. Which figure is a triangular pyramid? _____

8. What do figures A, C, and D have in common? _____

9. How are figures C and D alike? _____

10. How are figures C and D different? _____

ACTIVITY 2

Nets

A **net** is a flat (two-dimensional) pattern that can be folded into a solid (three-dimensional) figure.

Practice Problems

1. Solid figures A, B, and C in the figure below can be made by folding net A, B, or C on the Nets-1 worksheet. Figure out which net matches each figure.

a. **Think!**

- Figure A is a cube with six square faces.
- Which net on the Nets-1 sheet has six square faces?

Answer: Net B matches figure A.

b. **Think!**

- Figure B is a pyramid with four triangular faces and a square base.
- Which net on the Nets-1 sheet has four triangular faces and a square base?

Answer: Net C matches figure B.

c. **Think!**

- Figure C has three rectangular faces and two congruent triangular bases.
- Which net on the Nets-1 sheet has three rectangular faces and two triangular bases?

Answer: Net A matches figure C.

2. Check your answers to problem 1 by cutting out the enlarged nets from the copy of the Nets-1 sheet and folding each net along the fold lines (dotted). Make all the folds in the same direction. Fold the tabs over their corresponding faces—tab A over face A, tab B over face B, and so on. Use tape to secure the tabs to the faces.

On Your Own

Use the Nets-2 sheet to solve the following problems.

1. Study the two nets and name the solid figures you think they will form when folded.

a. _____   b. _____

2. Check your answers by folding the nets to make solid figures.

Nets 1

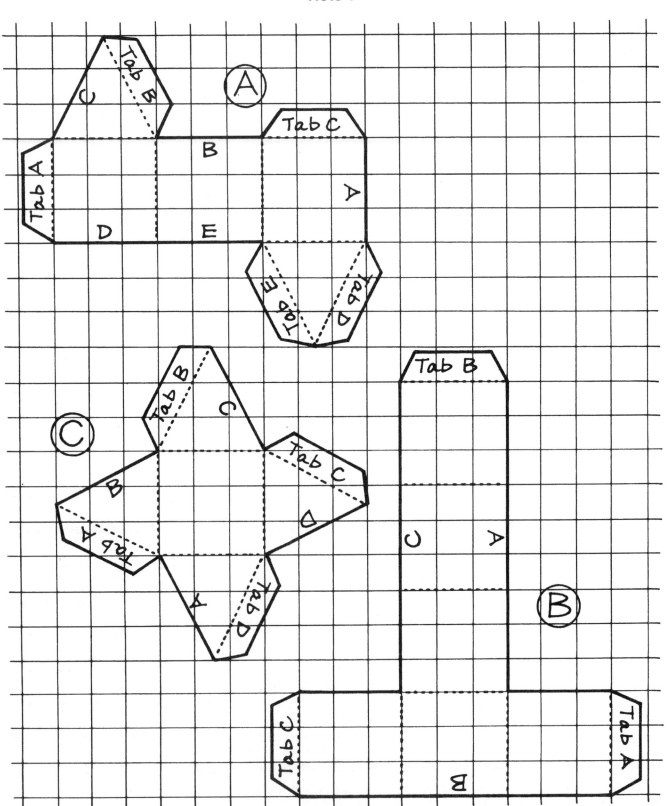

Nets 2

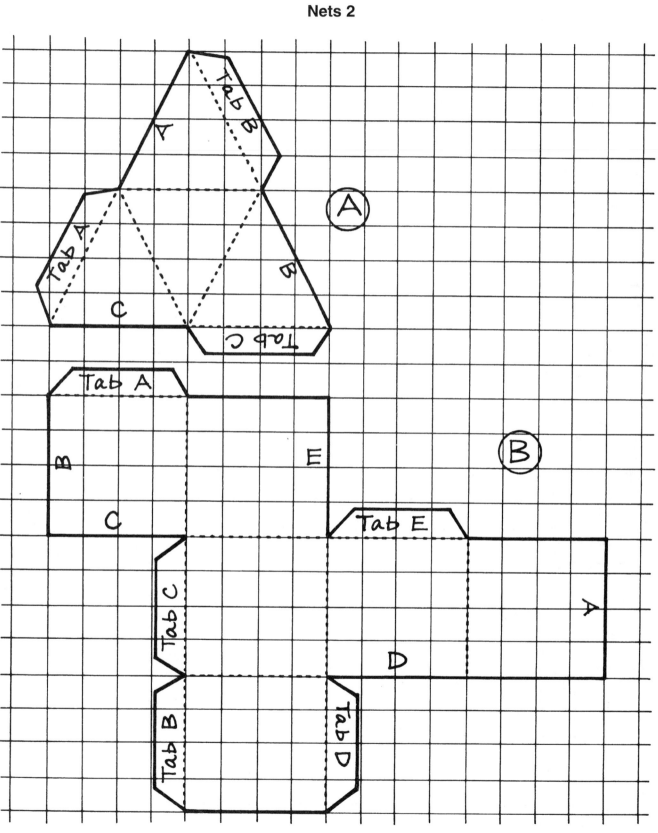

Coordinate Grids

TEACHING TIPS

Benchmarks

By the end of grade 5, students should be able to
- Describe the relationship between two sets of related data, such as ordered pairs in a table.
- Explain and record observations using graphs.

By the end of grade 8, students should be able to
- Prepare graphical representations of data.

In this chapter, students are expected to
- Use a coordinate grid to locate points and to identify the locations of points.
- Determine the value of ordered pairs and plot them on a grid.

Preparing the Materials

Activity: Coordinate Systems
- Make a copy of the Coordinate Systems activity sheet for each student.
- Make a copy of The Big Dipper grid sheet for each student.
- Make a copy of the Coordinate grid sheet for each student.
- Make sure each student has a calculator.

Presenting the Math Concepts

1. Introduce the new terms:

   coordinate grid A system of intersecting horizontal and vertical lines used to locate points.

   coordinates The parts of an ordered pair used in graphing.

   interval The fixed amount between the numbers on a scale.

   ordered pair A number pair that identifies the position of a point on a coordinate grid.

   origin The point where the *x*-axis and the *y*-axis of a graph intersect at a right angle.

   scale The marked intervals on *x*-axis or *y*-axis.

   ***x*-axis** The horizontal line of a grid or a graph.

   ***y*-axis** The vertical line of a grid or a graph.

2. Exploring the new terms:
   - The first coordinate in an ordered pair (2, 5) shows to move two spaces on the *x*-axis from the origin. In this chapter only positive numbers are used, thus the movement is to the right.
   - The second coordinate in an ordered pair (2, 5) shows to move five spaces on the *y*-axis from the origin. Again, only positive coordinates are used in this chapter, so the movement is up.

- When a 0 is part of an ordered pair, the 0 indicates no motion. For (0, 3), you do not move on the *x*-axis, but you do move up three units on the *y*-axis. For (3, 0), you move to the right three units on the *x*-axis, but you do not move on the *y*-axis.

EXTENSION

Cartographers (mapmakers) use grid lines on their maps and globes to help locate places on Earth. *Lines of latitude* circle a globe in an east-west direction and are measured north and south of the *equator* (latitude line around the center of Earth). On a flat map, they are the horizontal lines. *Lines of longitude* circle a globe in a north-south direction passing through both the *North* and *South poles* (points at the ends of Earth) and are measured in degrees east and west of an arbitrarily determined 0 degree longitude line called the *prime meridian,* which passes through Greenwich, England. On a flat map, they are the vertical lines. Coordinates on maps are generally listed with the latitude first followed by the longitude. Students can identify map coordinates for points and/or identify points from coordinates. You may wish to identify a specific city or a region. For example, have the students identify the country where they would find the coordinates (40°N, 5°W). The country is Spain.

ANSWERS

Activity: Coordinate Systems

A

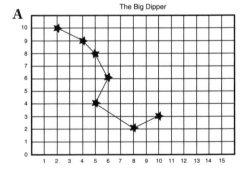

The Big Dipper

B

COORDINATE DATA

Point	Ordered Pair (*x, y*)	Point	Ordered Pair (*x, y*)
A	(6, 7)	F	(3, 4)
B	(2, 11)	G	(3, 3)
C	(2, 8)	H	(4, 1)
D	(3, 6)	I	(5, 1)
E	(4, 5)	J	(6, 3)

- A butterfly shape (antennae can be added to complete the diagram).

Name

ACTIVITY

Coordinate Systems

A **coordinate grid** is a system of horizontal and vertical lines used for locating points. The **origin** of a coordinate grid is the point where the x-**axis** (horizontal number line) and y-**axis** (vertical number line) intersect at a right angle. On the coordinate grid, this is the 0 point. The marked intervals on the x-axis and y-axis is called a **scale**. An **interval** is the fixed amount between the numbers on a scale. An **ordered pair** is a number pair that identifies the position of a point on a coordinate grid. **Coordinates** are the parts of an ordered pair used in graphing. The first coordinate in the pair shows how far to move along the x-axis of the grid from the origin, and the second coordinate shows how far to move along the y-axis of the grid from the origin.

Practice Problems

Look at the coordinate grid and answer the following:

1. What are the coordinates for point A?

2. What point does the ordered pair (2, 3) name?

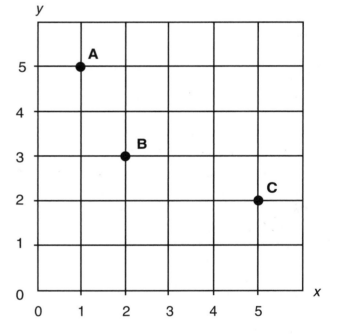

1. Think!

- Find point A on the grid, then follow a vertical line down to the x-axis scale. Read and record the number on the scale. This number is 1, and it is the first coordinate in the ordered pair for point A.

- Return to point A and follow a horizontal line to the y-axis scale. Read and record the number on the scale. The number is 5, and it is the second coordinate in the ordered pair for point A.

Answer: (1, 5)

2. Think!

- The first coordinate for the point is 2, which shows how far to the right from the origin the point is. Place your finger at the origin (point 0) and move to the right along the x-axis 2 spaces.

- The second coordinate for the point is 3, which shows how far up from the origin a point is. With your finger at 2 on the x-axis, move up 3 spaces. What is the name of the point?

Answer: Point B

28

ACTIVITY (continued)

On Your Own

A 1. Place a dot on the "The Big Dipper" coordinate grid for each of these ordered pairs.

Point	Ordered Pair	Point	Ordered Pair
A	(2, 10)	E	(5, 4)
B	(4, 9)	F	(8, 2)
C	(5, 8)	G	(10, 3)
D	(6, 6)		

2. Draw a star around each of the seven dots on the grid. Draw a line to connect points A through G. Note that the seven stars form what appears to be the bowl and handle of a ladle. A set of seven stars in the same positions as the stars on the grid can be found in the northern sky. Together they are called the Big Dipper and are part of a larger group of stars said to have the shape of a Big Bear.

The Big Dipper

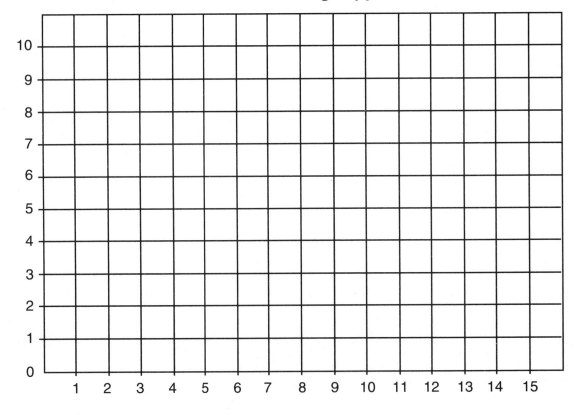

B 1. Use a calculator to solve each math problem in the Coordinate Data table.

2. Use the number answers for the *x* and the *y* coordinates to determine the ordered pair. Record the answers in the Coordinate Data table. In the example for point A, the ordered pair is (6, 7).

3. Place a dot on the Coordinate Grid sheet for each ordered pair for points A through J.

4. Use the pencil and the ruler to draw straight lines to connect the dots in the order listed from A to J.

5. Place a dot on the Coordinate Grid for each ordered pair for points K through X.

6. Use the pencil and the ruler to draw lines to connect the dots in the order listed from K through X, then draw lines to connect points A and K and points J and X.

7. What shape is produced? _____

8. Add any lines that might make the figure more complete.

Point	Ordered Pair (*x, y*)	Point	Ordered Pair (*x, y*)
K	(6, 8)	R	(10, 4)
L	(7, 8)	S	(10, 3)
M	(7, 7)	T	(9, 1)
N	(11, 11)	U	(8, 1)
O	(11, 8)	V	(7, 3)
P	(10, 6)	W	(7, 2)
Q	(9, 5)	X	(6, 2)

COORDINATE DATA			
Point	Coordinate for *x*-axis, ↔	Coordinate for *y*-axis, ↕	Ordered Pair (*x, y*)
A	$3918 \div 653 = 6$	$985 - 978 = 7$	(6, 7)
B	$23 - 21 =$	$6248 \div 568 =$	
C	$98 \div 49 =$	$357 - 349 =$	
D	$2001 \div 667 =$	$85 - 79 =$	
E	$23 + 45 + 21 - 85 =$	$36 - 23 + 56 - 64 =$	
F	$148 - 402 + 257 =$	$75 + 53 - 124 =$	
G	$7371 \div 567 - 10 =$	$14 \times 5 - 67 =$	
H	$(1072 + 400) \div 368 =$	$99 + 347 - 445 =$	
I	$234 + 85 - 314 =$	$321 + 78 - 43 - 355 =$	
J	$652 - 350 - 296 =$	$120 \div 60 + 1 =$	

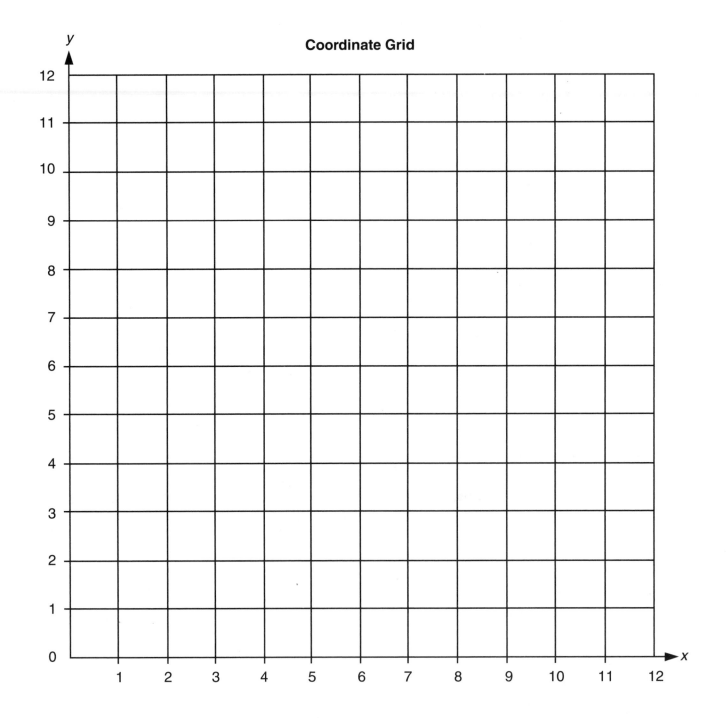

Coordinate Grid

Data Analysis and Probability

Data analysis is the systematic approach to separating the information (data) into its individual parts, examining those parts, and organizing them to solve a problem.

Probability is a measure of how likely it is that something will happen; it is the comparison of the number of ways a particular event can happen to the number of possible outcomes. One way to express probability is by using ratios and percents.

Counting Methods

TEACHING TIPS

Benchmarks

By the end of grade 5, students should be able to
- Use pictures to make generalizations about combining things and determining all possible combinations.
- Use multiplication to solve problems involving whole numbers.

By the end of grade 8, students should be able to
- Solve problems by organizing and interpreting data.
- Construct tree diagrams.
- Identify and apply mathematics to everyday experiences.

In this chapter, students are expected to
- Use tree diagrams and the Counting Principle to find all possible outcomes for a set of choices.

Preparing the Materials

Activity 1: Tree Diagrams
- Make a copy of the Tree Diagrams activity sheet for each student.

Activity 2: Line Plot
- Make a copy of the Line Plot activity sheet for each student.

Presenting the Math Concepts

1. Introduce the new terms:

   clusters Isolated groups of points on a line plot.

   Counting Principle A method of finding the total number of possible outcomes out of two or more possibilities by multiplying the number of different possibilities.

   gaps Large spaces between points on a line plot.

   graph A drawing that presents data in an organized way, showing relationships among sets of numbers.

   line plot A graph that shows data along a number line.

   outliers Data points on a line plot whose values are significantly larger or smaller than other values.

tree diagram A branching diagram showing all possible outcomes of a situation.

2. Explore the new terms:
   - A tree diagram looks like the branches on a tree. The structure of the tree shows all possible outcomes of a given situation.
   - A tree diagram can be used to list the outcomes for a combination of choices.
   - When dealing with the occurrence of more than one outcome, the Counting Principle can be used to determine the number of possible outcomes. For example, if a store sells hats in two colors and three sizes, all together there are $2 \times 3 = 6$ possible combinations of hats sold.
   - The Counting Principle can be used for two or more things or activities. For example, if four coins are tossed, how many arrangements of heads and tails are possible? There are two ways each coin can land: heads or tails. All together, there are $2 \times 2 \times 2 \times 2 = 16$ possible arrangements.
   - A line plot shows the distribution of values in a data set by stacking x's above each value on a number line.

EXTENSIONS

1. Students can draw tree diagrams with three or more choices.

2. *Permutation* is one of the ways to order a set of items. For example, given the set {1, 2, 3}, there are six permutations: {1, 2, 3}, {1, 3, 2}, {2, 1, 3}, {2, 3, 1}, {3, 1, 2}, and {3, 2, 1}. A factorial can be used to determine the number of permutations for the set. The factorial of a number is the product of all whole numbers from 1 to that number. The symbol for factorial is !. For the set of three numbers, the factorial would be $3! = 3 \times 2 \times 1$. Students can use factorials to determine the number of permutations for different numbers, such as 4! or 5!.

   $(4! = 4 \times 3 \times 2 \times 1 = 24; 5! = 5 \times 4 \times 3 \times 2 \times 1 = 120)$

ANSWERS

Activity 1: Tree Diagrams

1. a.

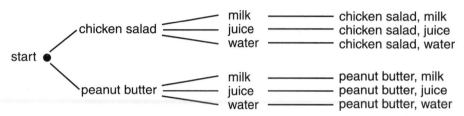

b. 6

c. $2 \times 3 = 6$

2. a.

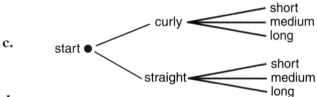

b. 6

c.

start ●

curly — short, medium, long
straight — short, medium, long

d. no

3. a. $3 \times 4 \times 3 = 36$

b. $4 \times 5 = 20$

c. $3 \times 2 \times 5 = 30$

Activity 2: Line Plot

a.

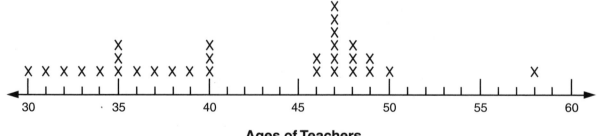

Ages of Teachers

b. 30

c. 58

d. 30 through 40; 46 through 50

e. between 40 and 46; between 50 and 58

Tree Diagrams

A **tree diagram** is a branching diagram showing all possible outcomes of a situation. The tree diagram below shows the possible types of hats sold by a store if the store sells two colors—red and blue—in three sizes—small, medium, and large. There are six possible hat combinations.

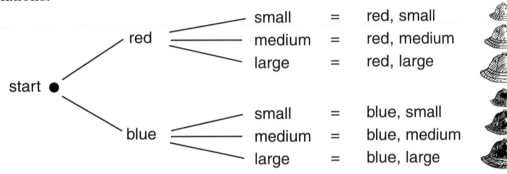

You can use multiplication to find the number of possible hat combinations by multiplying the number of possibilities for each item. This method is called the **Counting Principle**. In the hat example above, there were two color choices and three size choices. Using the Counting Principle, the possible hat combinations would be determined by multiplying the total choices of hat colors by the total choices of hat sizes: $2 \times 3 = 6$.

Practice Problems

1. David has two pairs of shorts (white and black). He has three shirts (blue, green, and red). How many different outfits can he make?

Think!

- From the starting point, draw a branch to each color of shorts.
- From each color of shorts, draw three branches to each shirt color.
- List the sum of each branch.

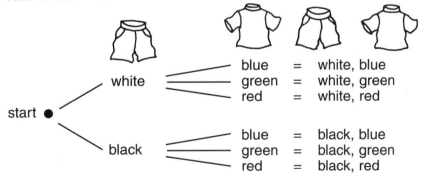

- Count the total combinations.

Answer: 6

Name

ACTIVITY 1 (continued)

2. Using the Counting Principle, how many different outfits can David make with two colors of shorts, three colors of shirts, and four colors of socks?

Think!

- Multiply the number of choices for each type of clothes being combined.

    $2 \times 3 \times 4 =$

Answer: 24

On Your Own

1. The school cafeteria has two choices of sandwiches (chicken salad and peanut butter) and three drinks (milk, juice, and water).

   a. If your meal is one sandwich and one drink, draw a tree diagram to show all the possible meal combinations.

   b. Using the tree diagram, how many meal choices do you have? _____

   c. Use the Counting Principle to determine how many meal choices you have.

   _____

2. Lauren is planning to change her hair style. She has a choice of three lengths (short, medium, and long) and two styles (curly and straight).

   a. Draw a tree diagram starting with the three hair lengths.

   b. How many different choices does Lauren have? _____

   c. Draw another tree diagram starting with the two hair styles.

   d. Are the combinations different than when you started with the three hair lengths?

   _____

3. Use the Counting Principle to find the number of outcomes in each situation.

   a. Dogs: 3 types, 4 colors, 3 heights. How many choices? _____

   b. Shoes: 4 types, 5 colors. How many choices? _____

   c. Cars: 3 brands, 2 models, 5 colors. How many choices? _____

© 2005 by John Wiley & Sons, Inc.

ACTIVITY 2

Line Plot

A **graph** is a drawing that shows data in an organized way. A graph shows relationships between sets of numbers. A **line plot** is a graph that shows data along a number line. A line plot uses stacked x's to show the distribution of values. The number of x's above each score indicates how many times each score occurred. Line plots allow special features, such as outliers, clusters, and gaps, to become more obvious. **Outliers** are data points whose values are significantly larger or smaller so that they are separated from the rest. **Clusters** are isolated groups of points. **Gaps** are large spaces between points.

Practice Problems

1. The table gives the high temperatures (°F) for one week in Dallas, Texas.

  a. Make a line plot of the data.

  b. Identify any outliers.

  c. Identify any clusters.

  d. Identify any gaps.

DAILY HIGH TEMPERATURE IN DALLAS, TEXAS (°F)						
Sun	**Mon**	**Tues**	**Wed**	**Thurs**	**Fri**	**Sat**
100	104	104	106	106	104	105

a. Think!

• Decide on a scale. Because the lowest temperature is 100 and the highest temperature is 106, choose a scale from 100 to 106. You can use an interval of 1 as shown in the figure.

• Place the temperatures in numerical order: 100, 104, 104, 104, 105, 106, 106.

• Mark an x for each data value on the number line.

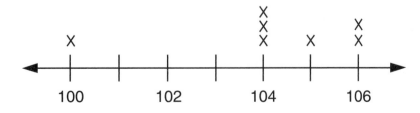

High temperature (°F) for one
week in Dallas, Texas

b. Think!

• Is there an outlier, a value that is separated from the rest?

Answer: 100°

c. Think!

• Is there a cluster, an isolated group of x's?

Answer: 104° through 106°

d. Think!

• Is there a gap, a space between temperatures?

Answer: between 100° and 104°

On Your Own

1. Suppose there are thirty teachers in a school. Their ages are 58, 30, 37, 36, 33, 49, 35, 40, 47, 47, 39, 32, 47, 48, 31, 50, 35, 40, 38, 47, 48, 34, 40, 46, 49, 47, 35, 48, 47, and 46.

a. Make a line plot of the data using the number line below.

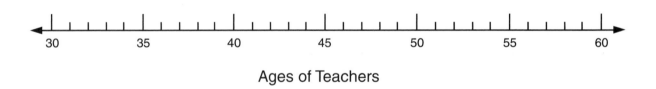

Ages of Teachers

b. What is the youngest age? _____

c. Identify any outliers. _____

d. Identify any clusters. _____

e. Identify any gaps. _____

Probabilities

TEACHING TIPS

Benchmarks

By the end of grade 5, students should be able to
- Express probabilities as fractions.

By the end of grade 8, students should be able to
- Determine the probability of a situation through experimentation.

In this chapter, students are expected to
- Use probability to describe how likely a particular outcome or event is to happen.
- Experimentally determine the probability of a baby being a boy or a girl.

Preparing the Materials

Activity: Probability
- Make a copy of the Probability activity sheet for each student.

Investigation: Boy or Girl?
- Make a copy of the Boy or Girl? investigation sheet for each student.
- Make a copy of the Probability Circles sheet for each student.
- Provide each student with 2 paper lunch bags.
- Provide 30 red kidney beans and 10 white lima beans for each student.

Presenting the Math Concepts

1. Introduce the new terms:

   event A particular outcome of an experiment or situation.

   experiment In probability, any activity that involves chance.

   probability The comparison of the number of ways a particular outcome can happen to the total number of possible outcomes.

2. Explore the new terms:
   - In a probability study, examples of experiments are rolling dice, tossing a coin, and spinning a spinner.
   - When rolling dice, rolling 2 or higher is one possible event.
   - A tree diagram looks like branches on a tree. The activity describes using a tree diagram to

calculate the probability of all outcomes from spinning two spinners. This example can be used to draw other tree diagrams to determine probabilities of events.

EXTENSIONS

1. Students can express the probabilities as fractions and as decimals.

2. The *Punnett square* is like a tree diagram in that it shows all the possible combinations. In science, the Punnett square is used instead of a tree diagram to show all the possible gene combinations that are transferred from parents to offspring. For example, consider the combination of genes from one parent with genes for pure brown eyes (BB) and the other with genes for hybrid brown eyes (Bb). Note that a pure trait (characteristic) has two identical genes while a hybrid trait has two unlike genes.

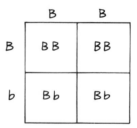

PUNNETT SQUARE

Offspring:
50% pure brown
50% hybrid brown
0% pure blue

Students can use Punnett squares to determine the probability of the traits for the offspring for each of the following combinations:

1. EE + Ee	3. HH + Hh
2. EE + ee	4. Hh + Hh

> Legend
>   EE   pure unattached earlobe
>   ee   pure attached earlobe
>   Ee   hybrid unattached earlobe
>   HH   pure brown hair
>   hh   pure red hair
>   Hh   hybrid brown hair

ANSWERS

Activity: Probabilities

1. a.

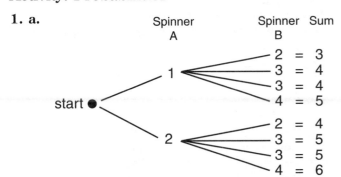

b.

Outcome Sums	Total of Each Outcome Sum	Probability for 8 Outcomes
3	1	1:8
4	3	3:8
5	3	3:8
6	1	1:8

ACTIVITY

Probability

Probability is the chance that something will happen. Probability is expressed as a ratio of the number of ways a particular outcome can happen to the total number of possible outcomes. In probability, any activity that involves chance is called an **experiment**. A particular outcome of an experiment or a situation is called an **event**.

Practice Problems

Look at the diagram of spinners A and B.

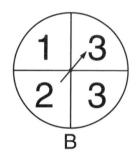

A   B

1. If each spinner is spun and the numbers from each are added:

a. Make a tree diagram to show all the possible outcomes.

Think!

- To make a tree diagram, start with all of the numbers on one of the spinners, such as A.

- For each of spinner A's numbers, list all of spinner B's numbers and connect each with a branch as shown.

- Add the numbers to show the sums of all the possible number combinations of spinners A and B as shown.

Answer:

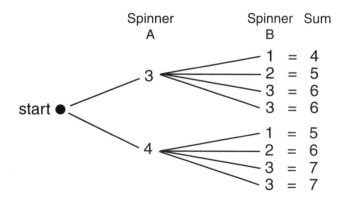

b. Express the probability of each outcome as a ratio.

Think!

- The probability of each particular sum is the ratio of the total outcomes of that sum to the total number of possible outcomes, which for spinners A and B is 8.

Answer:

Outcome Sums	Total of Each Outcome Sum	Probability for 8 Outcomes
4	1	1:8
5	2	2:8
6	3	3:8
7	2	2:8

On Your Own

Spinner A

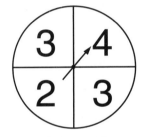

Spinner B

1. Look at the diagram below of spinners A and B. If each spinner is spun and the numbers from each are added:

a. Make a tree diagram to show the possible outcomes.

b. Prepare a table showing Outcome Sums, Total of Each Outcome Sum, and Probabilities for Outcomes. Express the probability of each outcome as a ratio with a colon.

INVESTIGATION

Boy or Girl?

PURPOSE

To compare experimental probability with the probability calculated using a tree diagram.

Materials

marking pen
2 paper lunch bags
30 red kidney beans
10 white lima beans
copy of the Probability Circles sheet

Procedure

1. Use the marker to label one bag RR and the other bag RW.

2. Place 20 red kidney beans in bag RR and 10 red kidney beans in bag RW.

3. Add 10 white lima beans to bag RW only and thoroughly mix the beans.

4. Stand the bags on a table.

5. Place the Probability Circles sheet on the table.

6. Without looking into the bags, take one bean out of each bag and place the two beans in circle 1 on the Probability Circles sheet. In the Bean Combination Data table below, mark an X in the box of the color combination for Circle 1, either RR (red/red) or RW (red/white). For example, if 1 red bean and 1 white bean

are placed in circle 1, an X is marked in that RW box.

7. Repeat step 6 until all the circles have one pair of beans in them and you have filled in all of the data table.

8. Using the experimental results, determine the probability (P) of each combination:

   • $P_{(RR)}$ = Total RR ÷ Whole (RR + RW) =

   • $P_{(RW)}$ = Total RW ÷ Whole (RR + RW) =

9. Complete the tree diagram below to show the possible combinations of the beans from the two bags.

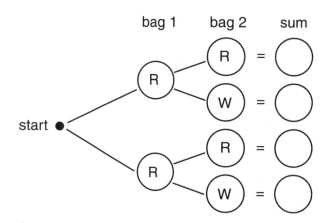

10. Using the tree diagram, determine the probability of each letter combination.

BEAN COMBINATION DATA					
Circle	RR	RW	Circle	RR	RW
1			6		
2			7		
3			8		
4			9		
5			10		

INVESTIGATION (continued)

11. Compare the experimental probabilities of each letter combination with the probability determined with the tree diagram.

Results

The tree diagram indicates that the probability of RR or RW combinations is 1 out of 2 or 50% RR and 50% RW. In this activity with only 10 trials, the results may vary from 50%. For example, the results shown in the example Bean Combination Data table show a ratio of 30% RR and 70% RW.

BEAN COMBINATION DATA					
Circle	**RR**	**RW**	**Circle**	**RR**	**RW**
1	X		6	X	
2		X	7		X
3		X	8		X
4		X	9		X
5	X		10		X

Total RR = 3   Total RW = 7
Whole (RR + RW) = 10

- $P_{(RR)} = 3 \div 10$
  $= 0.3$
  $= 30\%$

- $P_{(RW)} = 7 \div 10$
  $= 0.7$
  $= 70\%$

Why?

The *gender* (male or female) of a baby is due to two sets of instructions. One set of instructions comes from each parent. In probability, any activity that involves chance is called an experiment. In this experiment there are two possible combinations of instructions, RR and RW. RR in this experiment represents a female, and RW represents a male. In bag 1 (RR), there are only red beans; thus, only R instructions are possible. In bag 2 (RW), there are red and white beans; thus, two different kinds of instructions, R and W, are possible. If the combination is RR, a girl is produced. If the combination is RW, a boy is produced. While the tree diagram indicates the probability of a boy or a girl as 1 out of 2, the experiment shows that for any ten children born, this probability may or may not hold true. But the larger the number of children born, the more likely 50% will be boys and 50% girls.

© 2005 by John Wiley & Sons, Inc.

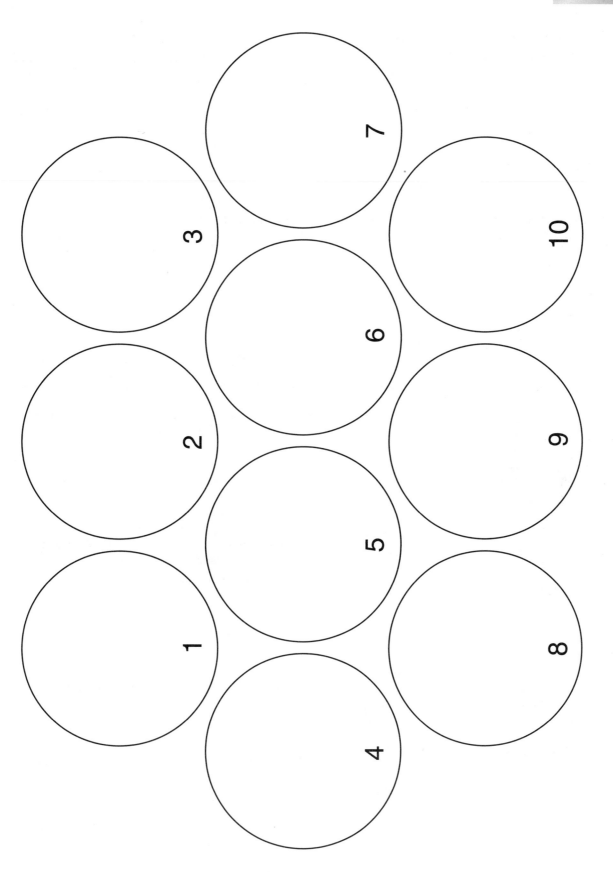

Probability Circles

Bar Graphs

TEACHING TIPS

Benchmarks

By the end of grade 5, students should be able to
- Use information from a bar graph in order to answer questions.

By the end of grade 8, students should be able to
- Construct bar graphs with and without technology.
- Use experimental results to make predictions and decisions.
- Use graphs and tables to solve problems.

In this chapter, students are expected to
- Construct and interpret bar graphs from given data.
- Solve problems by collecting, organizing, displaying, and interpreting sets of data on a bar graph.

Preparing the Materials

Activity: Bar Graphs
- Make a copy of the Bar Graphs activity sheet for each student.

Investigation: Heart Rate
- Make a copy of the Heart Rate investigation sheet for each student.
- Students can work in groups of three. The jobs of recorder, timekeeper, and pulse taker can be rotated.
- Make sure each group has a watch that can time seconds.

Presenting the Math Concepts

1. Introduce the new terms:

   bar graph A graph that uses vertical or horizontal bars to represent numerical data.

   data table A chart with data organized on it.

   graph title The title of a graph that represents the information presented on the graph.

2. Explore the new terms:
   - Graphs give a quick visual comparison of data. A graph is a drawing that shows data in an organized way.
   - All graphs should have (1) a graph title, (2) titles for the *x*-axis (horizontal) and the *y*-axis (vertical), (3) scales with numbers that have the same interval between each division, and (4) labels for the categories being counted.
   - Scales often start at 0, but they don't have to.
   - Bar graphs can have vertical or horizontal bars. The width and separation of each bar on the graph should be the same.
   - To read a vertical bar graph, find the top of the bar and then follow a horizontal line across to the scale. To read a horizontal bar graph, find the end of the bar and follow a vertical line down to the scale.
   - Some questions can be answered by simply comparing the lengths of the bars. For example, if a bar graph is used to compare the amount of rain for each month of the year, the month with the longest bar has the most rain and the one with the shortest has the least.

EXTENSIONS

1. Divide the class into two groups, one of boys and the other of girls. List the names of the girls in the class in a Girls Heart Rate Data table and the average number of heartbeats for each. List the names of the boys and their average number of heartbeats in a Boys Heart Rate Data table. Ask students to represent the heart rate data by making a bar graph with double bars representing data for boys and girls. Different-colored bars can be used to distinguish the data about boys from that of girls. Computer graphs can be prepared. Questions about the data tables and the bar graphs can be asked, such as:

   A group of adults have an average resting heart rate of 70 beats per minute. In your class:

   - How many boys have a higher resting heart rate than the adult group? How many girls?
   - How many boys have a lower resting heart rate than the adult group? How many girls?
   - What is the range of heart rates for boys? For girls?
   - What is the medium heart rate for boys? For girls?

2. Students can investigate the favorite brand of clothing of the students in their school. A random sampling of students can be made. For example, each student in the class can survey a predetermined number of students. The collected data can then be organized and a bar graph prepared.

ANSWERS

Activity: Bar Graphs

1. cheetah

2. three: cheetah, jackrabbit, and human

3. cheetah and jackrabbit

4. 12 mph (Answer may vary from 11 to 14 mph.)

5. 45 mph

Investigation: Heart Rate

Question	Answer
1	elephant, 25 beats per minute
2	rabbit, 200 beats per minute
3	The smaller the animal is, the greater its heart rate. Note: While information about three animals is not enough to determine a pattern, scientists have found that, generally, there is an increase in heart rate as the size of animals decreases.

Bar Graphs

Observations and/or measured facts are called data. A chart with data organized on it is called a **data table**. A graph is a drawing that shows data in an organized way. Graphs that use bars to represent data are called **bar graphs**. The **graph title** represents the information presented on the graph. The *x*-axis of a graph is the horizontal line with a scale or list of categories. The *y*-axis is the vertical line with a scale or list of categories. A scale is a series of numbers and units used to measure something, and an interval is the fixed amount between the numbers on the scale.

Practice Problems

Use the Animal Jumping Distances bar graph to answer the following:

1. What information does the graph represent?

2. What is the label on the *x*-axis?

3. What is the label on the *y*-axis?

4. What is the unit of measurement of the scale on the *y*-axis?

5. How far can the impala jump?

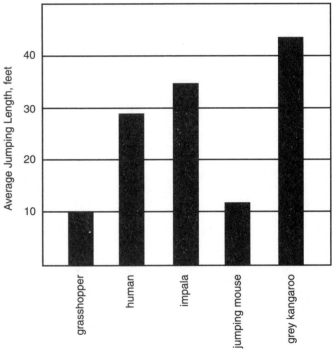

1. Think!

• What does the graph title tell you about the graph?

Answer: The graph is about how far the animals listed can jump.

2. Think!

• What is listed on the horizontal line at the bottom of the graph?

Answer: animals

3. Think!

• What is the label on the vertical axis of the graph?

Answer: average jumping length, feet

4. Think!

• A unit is an amount used for standard measurement, such as meter or pound.

Answer: The unit for the scale on the *y*-axis is feet.

5. Think!

- There are 10 divisions between each 10-foot interval, so each division is 1 foot.

- The top of the impala bar is in line with the fifth division past 30 feet.

Answer: The average jumping length of the impala is 35 feet.

On Your Own

Using data from the Animal Top Speeds bar graph, complete the Animal Top Speed Data table. Then use the completed table to answer the following questions:

ANIMAL TOP SPEED DATA	
Animals	**Speed, miles per hour**
cheetah	
jackrabbit	
human	
mamba snake	
red fox	

1. Which animal has the fastest top running speed? _____

2. How many animals run faster than the red fox? _____

3. Which animals can run faster than humans? _____

4. What is the speed of the slowest animal? _____

5. What is the top speed of the jackrabbit? _____

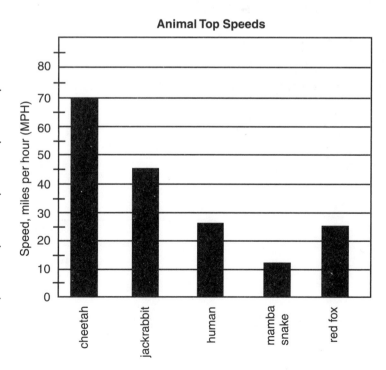

31
INVESTIGATION

Heart Rate

PURPOSE

To measure your heart rate and use a bar graph to compare it with the heart rates of other animals.

Materials

watch that measures seconds
pencil
helper

Procedure

(Note: Your heart rate should be measured during a time of inactivity, such as when you've been sitting for a while.)

1. Lay your arm on a table with the palm of your hand up.

2. Place the fingertips of your other hand below the thumb on your upturned wrist.

3. Gently press until you can feel your heartbeat. Note: You may have to move your fingertips around the area until you feel your heartbeat.

4. Ask your helper to be a timekeeper. When your timekeeper says "Start," count your heartbeats until the timekeeper says "Stop" at the end of 15 seconds.

5. Multiply the number of heartbeats counted in 15 seconds by 4, and record that number as the number of heartbeats in 1 minute (60 seconds) for trial 1 in the Heart Rate Data table.

6. Repeat steps 1 through 5 three times, recording the heartbeats per minute in trials 2, 3, and 4.

7. Average the four trials. (To get the average, add up the heartbeats and divide the total by 4.)

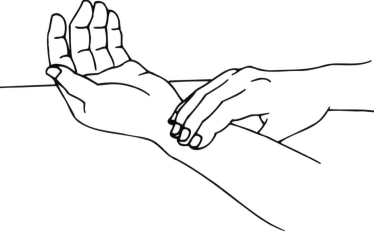

HEART RATE DATA					
	Trial 1	Trial 2	Trial 3	Trial 4	Average
Heartbeat/min					

8. Add a bar for your average heartbeat to the Animal Heart Rate graph. Use the bar graph to answer the questions below.

Animal Heart Rate

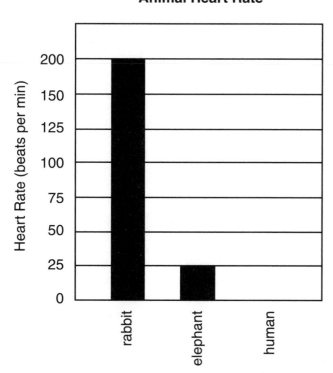

- Which animal has the least heart rate?
  _____

- Which animal has the greatest heart rate? _____

- The size of the animals from largest to smallest is elephant, human, rabbit. How does size affect heart rate?
  _____

- How does your heart rate compare to the average human heart rate on the graph? Lower? Higher? Equal?
  _____

Results

Heart rates can vary.

Why?

A steady beat is felt by the fingertips. The number of times your heart beats in one minute is called your heart rate. Each time the heart contracts, blood is forced through the *arteries* (blood vessels carrying blood away from the heart). The blood moves at a rhythmic rate, causing the arteries to pulsate, or throb. The beat you feel with your fingertips is called your *pulse*. The artery in your wrist is close to the surface of the skin, which is why you can feel your pulse there more easily.

Line Graphs

TEACHING TIPS

Benchmarks

By the end of grade 5, students should be able to
- Use tables of related number pairs to make a line graph.

By the end of grade 8, students should be able to
- Read and interpret line graphs.

In this chapter, students are expected to
- Interpret a line graph.
- Solve problems by collecting, organizing, displaying, and interpreting sets of data on a line graph.
- Measure plant growth and plot the average daily growth on a line graph.

Preparing the Materials

Activity: Line Graphs
- Make a copy of the Line Graphs activity sheet for each student.

Investigation: Sprouter
- Make a copy of the Sprouter investigation sheet for each student.
- Soak four pinto beans per student or group in water overnight. Keep the beans in the refrigerator to prevent souring.
- Any four different-colored pens can be used to draw the line graphs.
- If the stem growth for the plants is greater than 20 cm, the scale divisions can have a value of 2 cm each.
- Point out that the missing part of the scale as indicated by the zigzag line in the diagram is to be replaced with numbers from 4 through 18 on the *y*-axis and from 5 through 12 on the *x*-axis.

Presenting the Math Concepts

1. Introduce the new term:

    line graph A graph in which a line shows changes in data.

2. Explore the new term:
    - A line graph often shows how data changes over time.
    - Each point on a line graph represents one item of data. A line connects the points.
    - The points of some line graphs are ordered pairs made of two numbers, the first number is measured from the *x*-axis scale and the second from the *y*-axis scale.
    - A zigzag line can be used to show that part of a scale is missing. For example, graph for bean stem growth on page 188 of the Sprouter investigation. Point out that this is an example and that their graph should contain all the missing parts represented by the zigzag lines.

EXTENSION

How does the growth of different kinds of beans compare? Students can repeat the Sprouter investigation, numbering 8 places around the tape. Use two kinds of beans, such as pinto beans and lima beans. Alternate the beans in the cup, placing pinto beans beneath odd numbers and lima beans beneath even numbers. Use two different colors to prepare a line graph showing the growth of both beans.

ANSWERS

Activity: Line Graphs

1. January
2. four
3. October
4. 86°F
5. January, February, and December

Line Graphs

A graph is a diagram that shows the relationship between numbers or amounts. **Line graphs** use lines to show changes in data. The vertical height scale increases in value from bottom to top. So the lowest point on a line graph shows the least value. For example, on the candy graph, the height of each point represents the number of bars of candy eaten during the week. The days of the week are shown at the bottom from left to right.

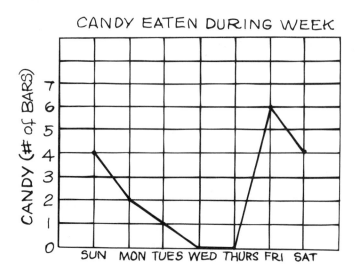

CANDY EATEN DURING WEEK

Practice Problems

Use the Average High Temperature, Washington, D.C., line graph to answer the following:

1. What do the *y*-axis and the *x*-axis represent?

2. What is the average temperature in February?

3. What month has the highest average temperature?

1. Think!

- The *y*-axis is the vertical number line with a scale measuring the temperature in °F.
- The *x*-axis is the horizontal line with a list of the months of the year.

Answer: The *y*-axis measures temperature in °F. The *x*-axis lists the months of the year.

2. Think!

- The interval between each number on the height scale is 10°F.
- There is one division between each number on the temperature scale. So the value of each interval (distance between each horizontal line) is 5°F.
- The dot for February is between 40° and 50°F.

Answer: The average temperature for February is 45°F.

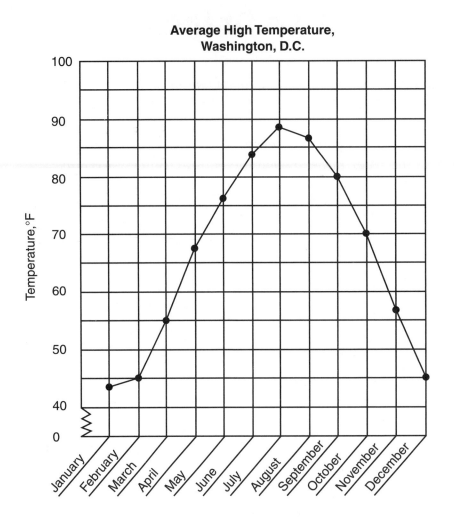

Average High Temperature, Washington, D.C.

3. Think!

• The highest dot on the line graph indicates the highest average temperature.

• Which month has the highest dot?

Answer: July has the highest average temperature on the line graph.

On Your Own

Use the Average High Temperature, Washington, D.C., line graph to answer the following:

1. Which month has the lowest average temperature? _____

2. How many months have an average temperature higher than May's? _____

3. Which month has a higher average temperature, April or October? _____

4. What is the average temperature for August, 84°F or 86°F? _____

5. Which months have a lower average temperature than March? _____

Sprouter

PURPOSE

To measure and graph the growth of a bean plant.

Materials

3 paper towels
10-ounce (300-mL) transparent plastic cup
masking tape
pencil
4 pinto beans that have been soaked
    overnight
tap water
metric ruler
1 sheet of graph paper
4 pens: red, black, green, and blue

Procedure

1. Fold a paper towel in half and use it to line the inside of the cup.

2. Crumple the other two paper towels and stuff them into the cup to hold the paper lining snugly against the sides of the cup.

3. Place a strip of masking tape around the outside of the cup and use the pencil to mark the tape with the letters A, B, C, and D. Space the letters evenly around the perimeter of the cup.

4. Place one pinto bean between the cup and the folded paper towel under each letter.

5. Moisten the paper towels in the cup with water. Keep the paper towels in the cup moist, but not dripping wet, during the entire experiment.

6. Observe the plant daily or as often as possible for 14 days. For each day's observation, measure the growth of the stem of each bean in centimeters from the top of the masking tape to the bottom of the seed leaves as shown. Record the growth of the stem in the Bean Stem Growth Data table. Day 1 is the starting day, and the growth is 0 cm. Note: It may take 4 or more days for measurable growth.

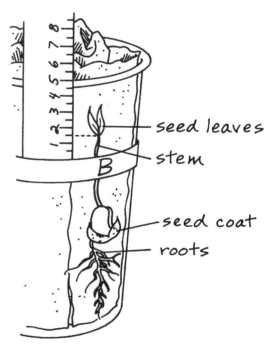

7. Title the graph paper "Bean Stems Daily Growth."

8. Prepare a line graph for plant A on the graph paper. Label the *y*-axis of the graph "Stem Growth, cm" and number each division from 0 through 20.

9. Label the *x*-axis of the graph "Days" and number the scale 1 through 14 as shown in the example on page 186.

BEAN STEM GROWTH DATA														
Bean Stem Growth, cm														
Plant	Day													
	1	2	3	4	5	6	7	8	9	10	11	12	13	14
A														
B														
C														
D														

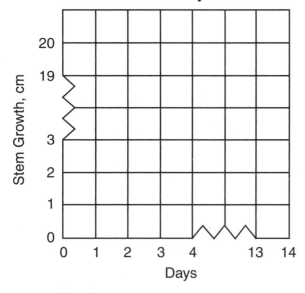

Plant A:
Bean Stem Daily Growth

a. Which seed started growing first?

_____

b. How long did it take each seed to start to grow? _____

c. Which plant had the greatest growth?

_____

Results

The time for the growth of the seed and the height of the plants will vary as will the line graphs produced. However, all of the line graphs for growing sprouts should show an increase in length over time.

Why?

The process by which a seed *sprouts* (begins to grow) or develops is called *germination.* The time it takes for a seed to grow is called its *germination time.* Since the same kind of seeds were used, the germination time for each seed will vary by only a few days. The height of each stem depends on when the seed starts to grow. If grown under the same conditions and given enough time, the stem growth of different plants generally will have only slight differences.

10. With the red pen, place dots on the graph for the daily growth of plant A. Use the pen and ruler to draw lines connecting the dots.

11. Repeat steps 8 through 10 three times drawing lines for the remaining plant on the same graph paper as used for plant A. Use a different-color pen for each plant.

12. Use the line graphs for the four plants to answer the following questions:

Mean

TEACHING TIPS

Benchmark

By the end of grade 5, students should be able to
- Measure to solve problems including the mean for a set of data.
- Use tables to solve problems.

By the end of grade 8, students should be able to
- Describe a set of data using mean.
- Use experimental results to make predictions.

In this chapter, students are expected to
- Measure lengths and determine the mean lengths of different groups.

Preparing the Materials

Investigation 1: Arm Length
- Make a copy of the Arm Length investigation for groups of 4.
- Groups of exactly 4 are needed. If a group has fewer than 4 students, they can use the arm length of a student from another group to complete their data.
- Cut one 4-meter piece of string for each group.

Investigation 2: How Long?
- Make a copy of the How Long? investigation sheet for each student.
- Provide 20 cooked or raw peanuts in their shell for each student or group. (CAUTION: If any students are allergic to peanuts, measure means of other objects.)

Presenting the Math Concepts

1. Introduce the new terms:

   average Mean; see below.

   mean The answer when the sum of a set of numbers is divided by the number of addends; average.

2. Explore the new terms:
   - Each number added is called an addend. When the numbers 2, 3, and 4 are added, there are three addends.
   - Mean is the same as average. For example, the average of the numbers 2, 3, and 4 is the sum of the numbers ($2 + 3 + 4 = 9$) divided by the number of addends (3). Thus the average or mean is $9 \div 3 = 3$.

- Means or averages give general information about collected facts. The mean snowfall for a year does not tell the snowfall on any specific day, but it does provide the information needed to compare snowfall from year to year. Because snowfall melts and fills lakes and reservoirs, the year-to-year comparison can give an indication of an area's dryness.
- Grades on school reports are a mean grade of scores in each subject during a specific time period.

EXTENSIONS

1. List the mean arm length average of each group on the chalkboard. Students can use this information to calculate the class's mean arm length.

2. Students can discover the effect of an outlier (number in a data set that is very different from the rest of the numbers) on the mean of a data set. Tables of data can be provided, and the mean with and without the outlier can be determined. For example, the outlier in the Daily High Temperature Data table is 45°F. The mean with the outlier is 82.9°F. The mean without the outlier is 89°F. Students can further research to discover how outliers affect the median and the mode of data information.

DAILY HIGH TEMPERATURE DATA (°F)	
Monday	87°F
Tuesday	88°F
Wednesday	90°F
Thursday	92°F
Friday	88°F
Saturday	90°F
Sunday	45°F

33

Arm Length

PURPOSE

To determine the mean arm length of a group.

Materials

pencil
4-meter piece of string
marker
scissors
meterstick
group of 4 people

Procedure

1. Write the names of each group member in the Actual Arm Length Data table.

2. Have one person hold his or her arm out to the side and have another person use the string to measure the first person's arm length. Starting at one end of the string, measure from the tip of the middle finger to the top of the arm. Mark the arm length on the string.

3. Use the meterstick to measure the length marked on the string to the nearest one-tenth centimeter. Record this measurement in the Actual Arm Length Data table under the student's name.

4. Repeat steps 2 and 3, beginning at the last mark to measure each person's arm length until all four have been measured. Cut the string at the last measurement.

5. Determine the sum of the four arm lengths. Record the sum to the nearest one-tenth in the data table.

6. Calculate the mean arm length by dividing the sum of the arm lengths by the total number of arms measured, which is 4. Record the value to the nearest one-tenth in the data table.

7. The whole string models the sum of the arm lengths of the group. Measure the entire string and record it as arm length sum in the Model Arm Length Data table.

© 2005 by John Wiley & Sons, Inc.

ACTUAL ARM LENGTH DATA

Students				Sum	Mean
Arm length					

INVESTIGATION 1 (continued)

How does the model arm length sum compare to the actual arm length sum?

8. Cut the string in half. Then cut each piece of string in half to form 4 equal-size strings. Each of these strings represents the mean arm length of the group. Measure one of the strings and record it as the mean arm length in the Model Arm Length Data table. How does this measurement compare to the actual mean arm length?

Results

The model and calculated arm lengths and mean arm lengths should be the same, although they may vary slightly due to rounding of numbers.

Why?

The **mean**, or **average**, is what you get when you divide the sum of a set of numbers by the number of addends. Addends are numbers added to find a sum. There were four addends in the actual measurement and in the model.

MODEL ARM LENGTH DATA		
	Arm Length Sum (length of string)	**Mean Arm Length (length of ¼ string section)**
Model		

How Long?

PURPOSE

To determine the mean length of a group of peanuts.

Materials

20 peanuts in the shell
ruler

Procedure

1. Measure and record the length of each peanut to the nearest inch.
2. Add the 20 length measurements together.

3. Determine the mean length by dividing the sum of the length measurements by the number of peanuts, which is 20.

Mean Length _____

Results

Results will vary.

Why?

The sum of the lengths divided by the total number of peanuts measured gives the mean length of the peanuts measured. Results vary because peanut lengths vary.

TEACHING TIPS

Benchmarks

By the end of grade 5, students should be able to
- Identify mathematics in everyday life.
- Find the median, mode, and range for an organized list of numbers.

By the end of grade 8, students should be able to
- Use median, mode, and range to describe data.

In this chapter, students are expected to
- Determine the median, mode, and range of numbers on a line plot.
- Measure reaction time and find the median, mode, and range of measurements.

Preparing the Materials

Activity: Median, Mode, and Range
- Make a copy of the Median, Mode, and Range activity sheet for each student.

Investigation: OOPS!
- Make a copy of the OOPS! investigation sheet for each student.
- Students should work in pairs, with one student testing the other's reaction times, then switching places to test the other student's reaction times.

Presenting the Math Concepts

1. Introduce the new terms:

   median The middle number when a list of numbers are ordered.

   mode The number that occurs most often in a list of numbers.

   range The difference between the lowest and highest numbers in a list of numbers.

2. Explore the new terms:
   - Some lists of numbers, such as 3, 4, 5, 7, 10, 12, do not have a mode.
   - If there is an even amount of numbers in a list, the average of the two center numbers is the median. For example, $5 + 7 \div 2 = 6$ is the median for the list of numbers 3, 4, 5, 7, 10, 12.

- The range is calculated by subtracting the least number from the greatest number. For the list 3, 4, 5, 7, 10, 12, the range is $12 - 3 = 9$.
- An x is used to represent one item on a line plot.
- A line plot helps to find the least and greatest numbers as well as the number with the most x's. (Review chapter 29 in this book for line plots.)

EXTENSIONS

1. Students can record the number of candy bars they eat during one week, collect this data for the class, and prepare a line plot of candy bars eaten by the whole class. Using the line plot, they can determine the median, mode, and range of candy bars eaten by the class.

2. Based on the results of the OOPS! investigation, students can prepare a data chart with the reaction distance of each student. Students can use this to determine the mode, median, and range of the reaction distances for the class. Using the range, determine if practice changes the reaction time.

ANSWERS

Activity: Median, Mode, and Range

1.

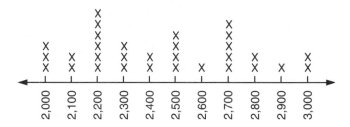

Number of Calories Eaten in 31 Days

2. 2,400 cal

3. 2,200 cal

4. $3,000 - 2,000 = 1,000$ cal

Median, Mode, and Range

The **median** is the middle number when a list of numbers are ordered. The **mode** is the number that occurs most often in a list of numbers. The **range** is the difference between the least and greatest numbers in a list of numbers.

Practice Problems

For the list of heights below:

1. draw a line plot

2. identify the median height

3. identify the mode of the heights

4. identify the range of the heights

Student Heights, cm
120, 120, 120, 130, 135, 140, 140, 140, 140, 150, 155, 160, 160

1. Think!

- Decide on a scale. Because the lowest height is 120 cm and the tallest height is 160, choose a scale between 120 and 160. You can use an interval of 5, as shown in the figure.
- Draw a straight line and label it with what is being counted and with the units it is being counted in.
- Label the range of heights on the line.
- Fill in x's for each student's particular height.

Answer:

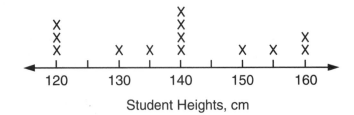

Student Heights, cm

2. Think!

- There are 13 heights. The median height will be the seventh number in the ordered list.

Answer: 140 cm

3. Think!

• On the line plot, which of the numbers has the most number of x's?

Answer: 140 cm

4. Think!

• The least height is 120 cm, and the greatest height is 160 cm. The difference between these numbers is 160 cm – 120 cm = ?

Answer: 40 cm

On Your Own

From the list of calories below:

1. Draw a line plot.

2. Identify the median calories eaten. _____

3. Identify the mode of the calories eaten. _____

4. Identify the range of the calories eaten. _____

Number of Calories Eaten in 31 Days
2000, 2000, 2000, 2100, 2100, 2200, 2200, 2200, 2200, 2200, 2200, 2300, 2300, 2300, 2400, 2400, 2500, 2500, 2500, 2500, 2600, 2700, 2700, 2700, 2700, 2700, 2800, 2800, 2900, 3000, 3000

OOPS!

PURPOSE

To measure reaction times and determine its mode, median, and range.

Material

table and chair
helper
yardstick (meterstick)

Procedure

1. Sit on the chair with your forearm on the tabletop and your writing hand extending over the edge.

2. Ask your helper to hold the measuring stick so that the bottom of the stick (the 0 end) is just above your hand.

3. Place your thumb and index finger on either side of, but not touching, the bottom of the ruler.

4. Ask your helper to drop the ruler through your fingers without telling you when it is going to be dropped.

5. After the ruler is released, try to catch it as quickly as possible between your thumb and fingers.

6. Observe the number on the ruler just above your thumb. Record this number as the reaction distance in the Reaction Distance Data table.

7. Repeat steps 1 through 6 nine times.

8. Use the data collected to prepare a line plot. From the line plot determine the median, mode, and range of reaction distances and record your answers.

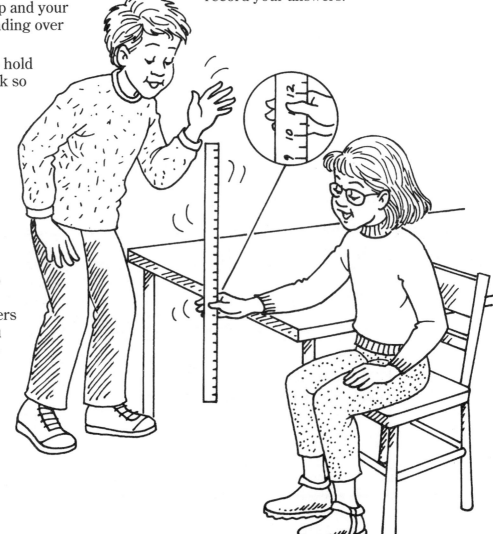

REACTION DISTANCE DATA			
Trial	Reaction Distance, inch (cm)	Trial	Reaction Distance, inch (cm)
1		6	
2		7	
3		8	
4		9	
5		10	

LINE PLOT

Use the line plot to determine the following for the reaction distances:

- **median** _____

- **mode** _____

- **range** _____

Results

The distance the ruler falls varies with each individual, thus the median, mode, and range of reaction distances will vary.

Why?

Reaction time is how long it takes you to respond to a situation. In this investigation, your reaction time was how long it took you to catch the falling ruler. In this investigation, the reaction distance is used to indicate reaction time. The greater the reaction time, the greater the reaction distance.

Glossary

acute angle   An angle that measures less than 90°.

acute triangle   A triangle in which all the angles are less than 90°.

addends   Numbers that are added together.

addition   The operation of adding together two or more numbers called addends which are combined into a resulting number called a sum.

adjacent   Adjoining sides.

algebra   The branch of mathematics in which arithmetic relations are explored using signs and letters to represent numbers.

algebraic equation   An equation with a variable.

algebraic expression   A mathematical phrase made up of variables and/or constants and one or more operational symbols; a combination of constants and variables and one or more operational symbols, such as $n + 2$ or $n \times 4$.

analyze   To separate information into its individual parts, examine those parts and organize them to solve a problem.

angle   The distance between two rays having the same endpoint; two intersecting line segments.

area   The amount of surface a figure covers.

average   *See* mean.

bar graph   A graph that uses vertical or horizontal bars to represent numerical data.

base   On a plane figure, the distance across the bottom. Also, the bottom of a solid figure; the parallel faces of a prism or cylinder.

base number   In reference to an exponent, it is a number multiplied by itself the number of times equal to the value of the exponent.

Celsius degree (°C)   A metric unit of measuring temperature.

Celsius scale   A metric temperature scale in which the freezing point of water is 0° and the boiling point is 100°.

chord   A straight line that begins and ends on a circle.

circle   A plane figure whose points are all the same distance from its center.

circle graph   A graph in the form of a circle that is divided into sections showing how the whole is broken into parts.

circumference   The perimeter of a circle.

clockwise   Rotation in the direction of the hands of a clock as viewed from the front or above.

clusters   Isolated groups of points on a line plot.

commutative property for addition   When numbers are added, the order of the addends may be changed without changing the sum.

cone   A solid that has curved sides and one circular base.

congruent   Equal in shape or size.

constant   A quantity whose value does not change.

conversion factor   A fraction equal to 1, whose numerator and denominator represent the same quantity but use different units.

coordinate grid   A system of intersecting horizontal and vertical lines used to locate points.

coordinates   The parts of an ordered pair used in graphing.

counterclockwise   Rotation in the opposite direction of the hands of a clock as viewed from the front or above.

Counting Principle   A method of finding the total number of possible outcomes out of two or more possibilities by multiplying the number of different possibilities.

cube   A rectangular prism whose faces are six congruent squares; a square prism.

cylinder   A solid figure that has curved sides and two congruent circular bases.

data   Observations and/or measured facts.

data analysis   The systematic approach to separating the information (data) into its individual parts, examining those parts, and organizing them in order to solve a problem.

data table   A chart with data organized on it.

decimal   A number that uses a decimal point to show tenths, hundredths, thousandths, and so on.

decimal point   A dot placed between the ones place and the tenths place in decimals.

degree (°)   (1) The unit of measuring temperature. (2) The unit of measuring an angle.

denominator   The number below the line in a fraction; the total number of equal parts in the whole.

diameter   A chord that passes through the center of a circle.

dividend   A number that is divided in a division problem.

divisible   A number that can be divided by another number without leaving a remainder.

division   An operation that tells how many groups there are or how many are in each group.

division bar   The line separating the numerator and the denominator in a fraction.

divisor   The number by which a dividend is divided.

edge   A line segment where two faces of a solid figure come together.

English system   A system of measurements based on the units foot, pound, pint, and second.

equal (=)   Symbol used to show that numbers or expressions are equal.

equation   A mathematical sentence that uses an equal symbol to show that two expressions are equal.

equilateral triangle   A triangle with three congruent sides.

equivalent decimals   Decimals that name the same amount.

event   A particular outcome of an experiment or situation.

experiment   In probability, any activity that involves chance.

exponent   A number to the right and above a base number that tells how many times the base is being multiplied by itself.

expression   Numbers or letters or numbers and letters combined with one or more operational symbols; see **algebraic expression** and **numerical expression**.

face   A flat surface of a solid.

factors   Numbers multiplied together to obtain a product.

Fahrenheit degree (°F)   An English unit of measuring temperature.

Fahrenheit scale   An English temperature scale in which the freezing point of water is 32° and the boiling point is 212°.

flip   To turn a plane figure over.

foot (ft)   An English unit of measuring distance equal to 12 inches and 0.3 meter.

force   A push or a pull.

formula   A rule represented by an equation that shows relationships between or among quantities.

fraction   A number used to express part of a whole and made up of two numbers separated by a line.

gaps   Large spaces between points on a line plot.

geometry   The study of shapes and figures.

gram (g)   Basic metric unit for measuring mass.

graph   A drawing that shows data in an organized way; relationships between sets of numbers.

graph title   The title of a graph that represents the information presented on the graph.

gravity   The force of attraction between objects in the universe; the force that pulls things on or near Earth's surface toward the center of Earth.

greater than (>)   Symbol meaning "is greater than."

height   In reference to a plane or solid figure, it is the distance perpendicular to the base of the figure.

hundredth   One out of 100 equal parts of a whole; the second place after a decimal point.

intersect   To cross or meet at a single point.

interval   The fixed amount between the numbers on a scale.

inverse operations   Operations that will undo each other. Addition and subtraction as well as multiplication and division are inverse operations.

isosceles triangle   A triangle with two congruent sides.

length   The measurement from one point to another. For a solid figure, it is the longest base measure.

less than (<)   Symbol meaning "is less than."

line   A straight path that can go on forever in either or both directions; a mark made by a pen, a pencil, or other tool on a surface.

line graph   A graph in which a line shows changes in data.

line plot   A graph that shows data along a number line.

line segment   A part of a line with two endpoints.

line of symmetry   The line along which a figure can be folded into congruent halves.

liter (L)   Basic metric unit for measuring volume.

mass   The amount of matter making up an object.

mean   The answer when the sum of a set of numbers is divided by the number of addends; also called the average.

measure   The process of finding the amount of something.

median   The middle number when a list of numbers is ordered.

meter (m)   Basic metric unit for measuring length.

metric conversion   The change from one metric unit to another.

metric system   A decimal system of measurements based on the units meter, gram, liter, and second.

mixed number   A number made up of a whole number and a fraction.

mode   The number that occurs most often in a list of numbers.

multiplication   An operation involving repeated addition.

net   A flat pattern that can be folded into a solid figure.

newton (n)   A metric unit of weight; 4.5 newtons equal 1 pound.

number   A symbol used to represent a quantity.

number line   A line divided into equal parts with one point chosen as the 0 point, or origin.

numerator   The number above the line in a fraction; the number of equal parts being considered.

numerical expression   Numbers combined with one or more operational symbols.

obtuse angle   An angle that measures greater than 90°.

obtuse triangle   A triangle in which one of the angles is greater than 90°.

operational symbols   Figures representing a math operation.

operations   Processes, such as addition, subtraction, multiplication, and division, that are performed on numbers.

ordered pair   A number pair that identifies the position of a point on a coordinate plane.

origin   Starting point; the point where the *x*-axis and *y*-axis of a graph intersect at a right angle.

ounce (oz)   An English unit of weight equal to $\frac{1}{16}$ pound.

outliers   Data points on a line plot whose values are significantly larger or smaller than other values.

parallel   Being equidistant apart at all points.

parallelogram   A quadrilateral whose opposite sides are parallel and the same length.

percent (%)   Per hundred. A way to compare a number to 100.

perimeter   The distance around a closed figure.

perpendicular   To intersect at a right angle.

pi   The ratio of the circumference of a circle to its diameter; π.

plane figure   A geometric figure that lies on a flat surface.

point symmetry   Characteristic of a figure if it looks unchanged after a 180° rotation.

polygon   A closed plane figure formed by three or more line segments that do not cross over each other.

polyhedron   A solid whose faces are polygons.

pound (lb)   An English unit of weight equal to 16 ounces.

power   Another name for an exponent.

prism   A solid figure with polygonal faces and two congruent parallel bases.

probability   The comparison of the number of ways an event can happen to the number of possible outcomes.

product   The number obtained after multiplying.

protractor   An instrument used to measure the size of an angle.

pyramid   A solid figure whose base is a polygon and whose faces are triangles with a common vertex.

quadrilateral   A four-sided polygon.

quantity   An amount or anything that can be measured by a number.

quotient   A number other than a whole-number remainder that is the result of division; the answer to a division problem.

radius (pl., radii)   A line segment from the center of a circle to any point on the circle.

range   The difference between the lowest and highest numbers in a list of numbers.

ratio   A pair of numbers used to compare quantities.

ray   A part of a line having only one endpoint.

rectangle   A parallelogram with opposite sides the same length and four right angles.

rectangular prism   A solid figure whose six faces are all rectangular.

reflection   The mirror image of a figure that has been flipped over a line.

remainder   The number less than the divisor that remains when division is finished.

rhombus   A parallelogram with all sides the same length and no right angles.

right angle   An angle that measures 90°.

right triangle   A triangle with one 90° angle.

rotation   A transformation that turns a figure around a point.

rotational symmetry   Characteristic of a figure if it looks unchanged after a rotation of less than 360°.

scale   A series of numbers used to measure something; the marked intervals on a graph's x-axis or y-axis.

scalene triangle   A triangle with no congruent sides.

solid figure   A geometric figure that has three dimensions and volume.

solution of an algebraic equation   The value of a variable that makes an equation true.

solve   To find the solution of an equation.

sphere   A solid figure that has no flat bases, and all points on its curved surface are an equal distance from its center.

square   A parallelogram with four equal-length sides and four right angles.

straight angle   An angle that measures 180°.

substituting   Replacing a variable with a known value.

subtraction   The operation that involves finding the difference between two numbers.

sum   The number that is the result of adding two or more addends.

symmetric figure   A figure that has one or more lines of symmetry.

temperature   A measurement of how cold or hot an object is.

tenth   One out of 10 equal parts of a whole; the first place after a decimal point.

thermometer   An instrument that numerically measures temperature.

thousandth   One out of 1,000 equal parts of a whole; the third place after a decimal point.

three-dimensional (3-D)   Having three measurements—length, width, height; said of solids.

ton (T)   A unit of weight equal to 2,000 pounds.

transformation   A change in the position or size of a figure.

trapezium   A quadrilateral with no parallel sides.

trapezoid   A quadrilateral with one pair of parallel sides.

tree diagram   A branching diagram showing all possible outcomes of a situation.

triangle   A three-sided polygon.

unequal sign (≠)   A sign used to show that the two parts of an equation are not equal.

unit   An amount used as a standard of measurement.

variable   A quantity whose value changes. A letter is often used to represent a variable.

vertex   The point where rays, line segments, or lines intersect; also called a corner; the point where two or more edges of a solid figure meet.

volume   The amount of space taken up by an object or enclosed by the object; the amount a container can hold.

weight   The measure of gravity pulling on an object.

whole numbers   Counting numbers and 0.

width   For a solid figure it is the shortest base measure.

word problem   A math problem using only words; a problem written in sentence form that needs to be solved using math.

x-axis   The horizontal line of a grid or a graph with a scale or list of categories.

y-axis   The vertical line of a grid or a graph with a scale or list of categories.

Index

pi (π)
  calculator key, 121
  definition, 117, 118, 198
  investigation, 120
plane, 89
plane figure, 87, 106, 107, 198
point symmetry, 144, 145, 198
polygon, 106, 107, 198
polyhedron, 135, 136, 199
positive numbers, 8
pound (lb), 73, 75, 199
power, 28, 121, 122, 199
prime meridian, 156
prism, 149, 151, 199
probability
  activity, 171–172
  definition, 161, 169, 171, 199
  investigation, 173–174
  teaching tips, 169–170
product, 14, 16, 199
protractor
  activities, 104–105
  definition, 101, 104, 199
pulse, 180
Punnett square, 169
pyramid, 149, 151, 199

quadrilateral
  activities, 112–116
  definition, 110, 112, 199
  teaching tips, 110–111
quantity
  activities, 51
  definition, 5, 49, 51, 199
quotient, 22, 24, 199

radius (pl. radii), 117, 118, 199
range
  activities, 192–193
  definition, 191, 192, 199
  investigation, 194–195
  teaching tips, 191
ratio
  definition, 44, 45, 199
  investigations, 45–46
rational numbers, 23
rays
  activities, 99–100
  definition, 98, 99, 199
  teaching tips, 98
reaction time, 194
real numbers, 23
rectangle
  area of, 126, 127–130
  definition, 110, 114, 199
rectangular prism, 149, 151, 199
reflection
  activity, 140–142

definition, 139, 140, 199
  investigation, 143
  teaching tips, 139
remainder
  decimal, 23
  definition, 22, 24, 199
  fraction, 23
rhombus, 110, 114, 199
right angle, 101, 102, 199
right triangle, 106, 107, 199
rotation, 144, 145, 199
rotational symmetry
  activity, 145–147
  definition, 144, 145, 199
  investigation, 148
  teaching tips, 144–148

scale
  definition, 156, 157, 199
scalene triangle, 106, 107, 199
scientific notation
  definitions, 28, 73–74
  negative, 73
  positive, 74
set, 23
signed numbers, 8
solid figure
  activities, 151–155
  definition, 87, 135, 136, 199
solution of an algebraic equation,
    54, 56, 199
solve, 54, 56, 199
South Pole, 156
sphere, 149, 151, 199
sprouts, 186
square, 110, 114, 199
star design, 96–97
straight angle, 101, 102, 199
substituting
  activities, 52–53, 56, 62
  definition, 49, 52, 56, 61, 62, 199
subtraction
  activities, 10–13
  definition, 7, 10, 199
sum, 7, 10, 199
supplementary, 111
symmetric figure, 139, 140, 199
symmetry, 139–143
  activity, 140–142
  horizontal line symmetry, 139
  investigation, 143
  line symmetry, 139, 140, 143, 199
  point, 144–147
  rotational, 144–148
  symmetric figure, 139, 140, 199
  teaching tips, 139
  vertical line symmetry, 139
temperature
  activity, 82–83

conversions, 81
  definition, 80, 82, 199
  investigation, 84–86
  measurement problems, 82–83
  teaching tips, 80–81
tenth, 27, 30, 199
thermometer
  definition, 80, 82, 199
  model, 84–86
thermoscope, 80
thousandth, 27, 30, 199
three-dimensional (3-D), 135, 136,
    199
ton (T), 73, 75, 199
transformation, 144–148
trapezium, 110, 112, 199
trapezoid, 110, 112, 199
tree diagram, 163, 165–166, 199
triangle
  activities, 107–108, 132–134
  acute triangle, 106, 107, 197
  area of, 131–134
  classification of, 107–108
  definition, 106, 107, 199
  equilateral triangle, 106, 107, 197
  investigation, 109, 134
  isosceles triangle, 106, 107, 198
  obtuse triangle, 106, 107, 198
  right triangle, 106, 107, 199
  scalene triangle, 106, 107, 199
  types of, 106–109

unequal sign (≠), 54, 56, 199
unit, 67, 69, 199

variable
  definition, 49, 51, 199
vertex (pl. vertices), 101, 102, 149,
    151, 199
volume
  activity, 136–137
  definition, 67, 69, 136, 199
  investigation, 138

weight
  activities, 75–76
  definition, 73, 75, 199
  investigation, 79
  teaching tips, 73–78
whole numbers, 7, 10, 199
width, 135, 136, 199
word problem
  activities, 12–13, 63, 75–78,
    123
  definition, 7, 12, 199

x-axis, 156, 157, 178, 199

y-axis, 156, 157, 178, 199